# BETHUNE
# IN
# SPAIN

"Here is Madrid, but never will it be fascist!"

"Through discipline the Republic defends itself."

# BETHUNE
# IN
# SPAIN

Roderick Stewart and Jesús Majada

McGill-Queen's University Press

Montreal & Kingston • London • Ithaca

© Roderick Stewart and Jesús Majada 2014

ISBN 978-0-7735-4383-6 (cloth)
ISBN 978-0-7735-9226-1 (ePDF)
ISBN 978-0-7735-9227-8 (ePUB)

Legal deposit second quarter 2014
Bibliothèque nationale du Québec

Printed in Canada on acid-free paper that is 100% ancient forest free
(100% post-consumer recycled), processed chlorine free

McGill-Queen's University Press acknowledges the support of the Canada
Council for the Arts for our publishing program. We also acknowledge the
financial support of the Government of Canada through the Canada Book
Fund for our publishing activities.


Library and Archives Canada Cataloguing in Publication

Stewart, Roderick, 1934–, author Bethune in Spain / Roderick Stewart
and Jesús Majada.

Includes newspaper articles, printed interviews, personal letters, and reports.
Includes bibliographical references, filmography and index.
Issued in print and electronic formats.
ISBN 978-0-7735-4383-6 (bound).
ISBN 978-0-7735-9226-1 (ePDF).
ISBN 978-0-7735-9227-8 (ePUB)

1. Bethune, Norman, 1890–1939. 2. Bethune, Norman, 1890–1939 –
Travel – Spain. 3. Spain – History – Civil War, 1936–1939 – Participation,
Canadian. 4. Spain – History – Civil War, 1936–1939 – Medical care.
5. Spain – Description and travel. 6. Physicians – Canada – Biography.
7. Philanthropists – Canada – Biography. 8. Communists – Canada –
Biography. I. Majada Neila, Jesús, author II. Title.

R464.B4S743 2014          617.092          C2014-900869-4
                                           C2014-900870-8


This book was designed and typeset by studio oneonone in Minion 11/14.2

# CONTENTS

"Evacuate Madrid."

# PREFACE

Jesús Majada Neila, writer and retired teacher of Spanish literature, lives near the city of Málaga in southern Spain. His principal interest, which has led him to write books and to design pictorial exhibitions, is the greatest tragedy of the Spanish Civil War: the flight of 100,000 unarmed civilians from Málaga along the Mediterranean coastal road to Almería, 200 kilometres to the east, in February 1937. Under attack by Spanish Nationalist land, air, and sea forces, and pursued by Italian Blackshirts, many of the refugees were slaughtered.

In 2006, in response to Jesús' suggestion, the University of Salamanca invited me to participate in a round table as part of *Las Brigadas Internacionales: 70 años de Memoria Histórica*, a conference held to mark the seventieth anniversary of the outbreak of the Spanish Civil War. During a conversation at the conference Jesús suggested that we collaborate on a book describing Bethune's achievements in Spain. The model he proposed was my *The Mind of Norman Bethune* (1977), in which I outlined Bethune's life using his own writings and photographs that others had taken of him. When Jesús pointed out that he had various unpublished photographs of Bethune, I became interested in his idea. Many of Bethune's writings in Spain had appeared in my book and, later, in Larry Hannant's *The Politics of Passion: Norman Bethune's Writing and Art* (1998). However, during our research for the then-unpublished *Phoenix: The Life of Norman Bethune*, Sharon Stewart and I had come upon unpublished letters and documents written by Bethune during his seven-month stay in Spain. What Jesús and I began to discuss that day evolved into this book, which contains the known writings of Bethune in Spain and a selection of photographs, including many published for the first time. Its first, Spanish, edition was published in Madrid by Fundación Domingo Malagón on 12 November 2009, the seventieth anniversary of Bethune's death. The publication of the present English-language edition in 2014 marks the seventy-fifth anniversary of Bethune's death. We offer it in tribute to Norman Bethune, a Canadian who was truly a doctor without borders.

RODERICK STEWART
Richmond Hill, Ontario

## EDITORIAL NOTE

Excerpts from Bethune's writings and radio broadcasts are reproduced in this volume as they appear in their originally published or manuscript form; Bethune's punctuation and spelling have been preserved, and omitted words have been supplied in square brackets. Some minor errors of spelling have been silently corrected.

On the way to Almería they machine-gunned us: my parents covered us
with their bodies. Nothing happened to us but there were victims on
the highway. Of course, I saw some of them. On the morning of my
birthday, an Italian seaplane bombed us in the town of Motril. I
remember it very well because one of its bombs hurled my uncle and
me into the air. Luckily we were in a recently ploughed field and the
soft earth cushioned us.

*Rosendo Fuentes, survivor of the flight from Málaga to Almería*


There was such great fear that if they made out a crow in the distance
they thought it might be a plane and fled in terror. I have never forgot-
ten that woman who, wounded by a shell, in the middle of a pool of
blood, was suckling and embracing her two-month-old son.

*Miguel Escalona Quesada, survivor of the flight from Málaga to Almería*

# BETHUNE
# IN
# SPAIN

Refugees on the Málaga–Almería road. (Hazen Sise. National
Film Board of Canada)

Spain, January 1937.

# 1 ◆ THE ROOTS

Norman Bethune always believed that his destiny was profoundly influenced by his ancestry: "I come of a race of men," he wrote, "violent, unstable, of passionate conviction and wrong-headedness, yet with it all a vision of truth and a drive to carry them on to it even though it leads, as it has done in my family, to their own destruction." Who, then, were this "race of men" called Bethune?

The name derives from Betunia, a region in the Roman province of Gaul (modern northwest France), and first appeared in a ninth-century document that referred to Robert, first lord of Béthune and Richebourg, and protector of the Church of Arras. Nearly 400 years later, not long after the first Béthune arrived in Scotland from the continent, various descendants rose to prominence as landowners, clergymen, and practitioners of medicine. Among them was Angus (b. 1540), first in a hereditary line of physicians appointed to serve the noted clan McLeod of Dunvegan on the Isle of Skye.

In the early 1770s, the Reverend John Bethune (1751–1815), a direct descendant, left Scotland for the English colony of North Carolina. Loyal to the Crown, after the American Revolutionary War he went north to British-controlled territory, where he would later be recognized as one of the founders of the Presbyterian Church of Canada.

Like some of their Scottish ancestors, several of John Bethune's descendants achieved distinction in various fields of endeavour. One of his sons became principal of McGill University in Montreal, another became the Anglican bishop of Toronto, and a third, Angus (1783–1858), rose to a leading position in the Hudson's Bay Company. His son, Norman (1822–1892), studied medicine in Edinburgh and London and returned to Canada to become a respected surgeon and professor of medicine at Victoria College, later part of the University of Toronto.

Malcolm Nicolson Bethune (1857–1932), Norman's second son, married an English immigrant, Elizabeth Ann Goodwin. Acting on the persuasion of his evangelical wife, Malcolm became a "born-again" Christian and was ordained in the Presbyterian Church in 1889. Their first son, Henry Norman, was born the following year in the small town of Gravenhurst, 150 kilometres north of Toronto, where Malcolm had gone to start his ministerial career.

Reverend Bethune was an outspoken individual willing to stand up for his principles and to openly criticize certain members of his congregations for not adhering to the high standards of Christian behaviour that he preached. As a result, he seldom remained long in any church, keeping himself and his family frequently on the move. By the time Norman graduated from secondary school at the age of seventeen, he had lived in six municipalities in Ontario. Unable to find roots in his youth, he would remain on the move throughout his life.

Like his father, Norman had an impatient nature, a quick temper, and a tendency to speak his mind freely – even when no one agreed with him. Highly intelligent, imaginative, and insatiably curious, he was daring and eager to succeed. But there was another side to his developing character. In his very early years his parents, inspired by evangelical Christian values, began to instill in him a desire to dedicate his life to the service of others. Only in this way, they told him, could he live up to the high standards of his ancestors. Before he reached his teens, Norman had decided to emulate his grandfather, Dr. Norman Bethune. He, too, would become a renowned surgeon.

Working in the northern woods in logging camps and with railway construction companies, he earned enough money to put himself through university. He was about to enter the third year of his medical studies at

Bethune (centre) – as Frontier College instructor – with other loggers near Georgian Bay, winter 1912. (Photographer unknown. Library and Archives Canada c-056826)

the University of Toronto when, on 4 August 1914, Great Britain declared war on Germany. Bethune immediately enlisted in the Canadian Army Medical Corps. At the Second Battle of Ypres in April 1915, he was serving as a stretcher-bearer carrying wounded from the trenches when he was struck by shrapnel in his left leg. Taken by his comrades to safety, he was treated and, several days later, transported to a hospital in England. After his convalescence, he was instructed to return to Canada to complete his medical training.

Bethune graduated at Christmastime in 1916 and joined the Royal Navy in the spring of 1917. As ship's surgeon he served aboard HMS *Pegasus*, one of the first aircraft carriers, on patrol in the North Sea. Near the end of October 1918, after treating more than half of the crew for "the Spanish flu," Bethune fell ill himself. Transferred to a hospital in Scotland, he lay critically ill for three weeks before beginning to recover in mid-December.

Demobilized in February 1919, Bethune obtained a six-month internship at the famous Hospital for Sick Children in London; when that expired he returned to Canada. In early 1920, he joined the fledgling

Canadian Air Force as its first Senior Medical Officer, but finding little challenge in his work he took a leave of absence in October and returned to Great Britain. Following in his grandfather's footsteps, he set about obtaining a fellowship in surgery in Edinburgh. There he met Frances Campbell Penney, the attractive daughter of a long-established Edinburgh family. Although keenly interested in courting her, he was obliged to return to London to take a hospital position to earn money while he prepared for his fellowship examinations. In London he met Isabelle Rosalind Humphreys-Owen, a widow and a member of the notable Sassoon family. While maintaining a correspondence with Penney in Edinburgh, Bethune entered into a romantic relationship with Humphreys-Owen, who began to finance a business that Bethune was trying to run in his spare time. Much attracted to art, he spent many hours in art galleries and in the company of artists whom he met in Soho, the bohemian quarter of London. With money supplied by Humphreys-Owen, he began to make trips to Portugal and Spain to buy paintings and *objets d'art*, which he hoped to sell at a profit in London.

Bethune returned to Edinburgh in October 1921 to make the final preparations for his examinations to allow him to become a Fellow of the Royal College of Surgeons. After passing the examinations in January, he returned to London to his hospital position and his art business. While in Edinburgh, he saw Frances frequently, and their romance blossomed. Six months later, she went to London to take a position in social work. Bethune remained involved with both women until the late spring of 1923, when Penney discovered that Bethune's interest in Humphreys-Owen went beyond business. Forced at last to choose between them, he assured Penney of his undying love and persuaded her to marry him at once. The marriage took place in August 1923. With money from a legacy Penney had recently inherited, they spent the next six months travelling through Italy and Switzerland, and also in France and Austria, where Bethune was able to take brief courses of study in surgery.

The couple soon ran out of money and returned to London in the spring of 1924. When he failed to find a hospital position, Bethune persuaded his wife that he could earn far more money in America. Frances reluctantly agreed to emigrate, and in October they arrived in the booming city of Detroit, at that time the automobile manufacturing capital of the world. However, the instant success that Bethune had expected eluded him. As they watched their funds dwindle and their debts increase, tension between Bethune and his wife grew. Frances loathed Detroit; they argued; and, when Bethune began to drink, the conflict escalated to the point where she left for several months to stay with a friend in Montreal.

Finally, Bethune made a breakthrough. He managed to obtain operating privileges in a leading Detroit hospital, and various doctors whom he met in the Detroit medical community began to send him patients requiring surgery. By the spring of 1926 his fortunes had changed. He paid his debts, bought an automobile, and moved with Frances to a luxury apartment, which was soon decorated with the numerous paintings he began to buy.

This period of good fortune did not last. Several months later, when Bethune found himself tiring easily, he consulted a medical colleague. Suspecting that he had contracted tuberculosis of the lungs, the doctor arranged for Bethune to have a chest x-ray. His diagnosis was confirmed. Just before Christmas of 1926, Bethune entered Trudeau Sanatorium in Saranac Lake, New York. Meanwhile, the lack of money to pay for Bethune's hospital costs and his wife's upkeep in Detroit led to renewed conflict between them. Finally, Frances Bethune decided to end their relationship. In the early winter of 1928, after obtaining a divorce decree requiring Bethune to pay her $25,000, she returned to Scotland.

Overcome by his abruptly altered circumstances, Bethune became depressed. When there was no sign of improvement in his health, he even devised a scheme to take his own life rather than succumb to tuberculosis. Yet he never quite gave up hope. Searching the sanatorium's medical library for information on tuberculosis, he came across the description of a treatment called artificial pneumothorax. This procedure consisted of pumping air through a hollow needle inserted through the skin between the ribs into the chest cavity outside the lung, causing the lung to collapse and allowing it to rest. Repeated periodically, the procedure could allow the damaged area to heal and prevent the spread of the disease to the rest of the lung. The discovery electrified Bethune, and he went immediately to the head of the medical staff to demand the treatment. The answer he received was a firm no. He was told that the procedure was extremely dangerous: the needle could puncture his lung, causing even greater damage. Bethune simply unbuttoned his shirt, exposing his chest, and said, "I welcome the risk."

The procedure was performed on 27 October 1927. The fears of the head of the medical staff proved well-founded; Bethune's lung was indeed punctured, putting his life in danger. But he made a rapid recovery and, six weeks later, was well enough to leave the sanatorium. The doctors believed that, by repeating the procedure every several weeks, they would likely restore his lung to its normal state of function.

The almost miraculous success of the process had a deep emotional impact on Bethune. Before he underwent this first pneumothorax treatment, he had spent many hours examining the first thirty-six years of his life. Although he had long since rejected his parents' religious beliefs, he still believed in the Christian values they had instilled in him, particularly with respect to helping those in need. During those hours of meditation he concluded that, in his selfish determination to become rich and famous, he had forsaken his duty to serve others, and in so doing had brought upon himself the disaster that had befallen him. He now believed he had been spared from death so that he might achieve some great good. "When I leave here I am going to do something that will benefit the human race," he told a fellow patient. He now set a high goal for himself: he pledged to dedicate his life to finding a cure for tuberculosis.

Acting on this inspiration, he wrote to the Canadian pioneer in tuberculosis treatment, Dr. Edward Archibald of the Royal Victoria Hospital and McGill University in Montreal. Archibald agreed to instruct him in the techniques of thoracic surgery. From 1928, when he became Archibald's assistant, until 1933, Bethune published a series of research papers in medical journals, won international recognition for his invention of surgical instruments, and became noted for his speed and skill as a surgeon.

He also tried to renew his relationship with his wife. Doubtful of her chances of happiness with Bethune, but very unhappy in Edinburgh, Frances finally gave in to his coaxing and remarried him in Montreal in November 1929. However, despite a promising beginning lasting several months, their marriage broke down again. In March 1933 they were divorced for the second time.

As his marriage was falling apart, so was his relationship with Dr. Archibald. Although he had some differences with his younger colleague,

Archibald recommended Bethune for a position at the Hôpital du Sacré-Cœur in Montreal, a francophone Roman Catholic institution. Despite his atheism and his inability to speak French, Bethune was accepted, and on 30 January 1933 he performed his first operation there as head of thoracic surgery.

Another phase of Bethune's life was starting to take shape at this time. His interest in art was rekindled, and after a few months of instruction by a well-known Montreal artist, Adam Sherriff-Scott, Bethune decided to paint on his own. He also started to visit art galleries in Montreal and soon became friendly with many members of the city's active art community. Through contacts with artists and writers, who spoke frequently of the unemployment and misery brought about by the Great Depression, he became interested in politics, a subject of which he knew very little. To the extent that he cared at all, he had always considered himself a right-wing conservative. Through conversations with his new friends, many of whom were left-wing in outlook, his political perspective began to change. One result was his recognition of the relationship between the huge number of unemployed workers and the rising incidence of tuberculosis in the province of Quebec, which was the highest in Canada. He remembered a saying of Dr. Trudeau, founder of the sanatorium at Saranac Lake: "There is a rich man's tuberculosis and a poor man's tuberculosis. The rich man recovers and the poor man dies."

Inspired by his belief that it could one day be eradicated altogether, Bethune began a crusade to curb tuberculosis. In speeches, he proposed and advocated for an extensive public education program involving increased training for medical students in the treatment of the disease, mandatory chest x-rays for all schoolchildren, and complete physical examinations for all nurses, nursemaids, and food handlers in Montreal. His ideas were sound, his critics agreed, but the only source of the large outlay of money required to put his proposals into effect was government. However, in the middle of an economic depression no government would consider adopting such a program.

Disappointed but not daunted by his failure to gain support for his ideas, Bethune decided to attend the fifteenth International Physiological Congress in Moscow in August 1935. His primary interest was not the sessions of the Congress, but to learn how the Russians dealt with tuberculosis. Although his visit lasted only a week, he returned convinced that the state-operated Soviet medical system was doing a far better job of treating the disease and curbing its spread than the privately run system in Canada. He returned to Montreal enthused by what he had seen and eager to talk about it. The mental leap from the Soviet medical system to the ideology on which it was based was short. In October, Bethune joined the Communist Party of Canada. At the time, the Communist Party was illegal in Canada, and the generally hostile attitude of most Canadians – and certainly the Roman Catholic administration of Sacré-Cœur – toward Communism made it absolutely essential that Bethune conceal his political commitment.

Bethune accepted the need to hide his party affiliation, but he was determined to take action consonant with his beliefs. In December 1935 he set up a small study group of left-leaning medical personnel and social workers to conduct research and draw up a plan for a medical system designed to serve all Canadians. Meanwhile, he continued to speak out in favour of characteristics that he admired in the Soviet medical system. In a provocative speech entitled *Take the Private Profit Out of Medicine*, which

En route to the Soviet Union, summer 1935.
(Photographer unknown. Roderick Stewart collection)

he gave to the Montreal Medico-Chirurgical Society on 17 April 1936, he summarized his attitude in the following sentences:

Socialized medicine and the abolition or restriction of private practice should appear to be the realistic solution of the problem. Let us take the profit, the private economic profit, out of medicine, and purify our profession of rapacious individualism. Let us make it disgraceful to enrich ourselves at the expense of the miseries of our fellow-men ... Let us redefine medical ethics – not as a code of professional etiquette between doctors, but as a code of fundamental morality and justice between Medicine and the people.

At the beginning of the summer Bethune learned that a Quebec provincial election would take place in August. Hoping to make medical care an election issue, he decided that this was the time to put together the research findings that he and his colleagues had been gathering since Christmas. They summarized their ideas in four plans that could be set up as pilot projects to improve the existing free-enterprise system, and sent them to the political candidates in the election and to all medical, dental, and nursing societies in the Montreal region. Bethune had agreed that none of the plans would advocate total government control: his colleagues had convinced him that their proposals were setting a precedent in Canada and that Canadians were not yet prepared for a truly socialized system.

The negative reaction to his April speech prepared Bethune for the medical profession's equally hostile reception to his group's proposals. As it happened, what distressed him was the indifference of politicians and of the general public. The scant newspaper coverage of the plans elicited neither a negative nor a positive reaction. No one seemed to care.

This rejection came at a low point in Bethune's personal life. He had been in several unsuccessful relationships since his divorce three years earlier. Then, in 1935, he had met and fallen deeply in love with Marian Scott, a painter. She loved him in return, but refused to end her marriage to the law professor and poet F.R. Scott. Now, in the summer of 1936, he was despondent and lonely. Restless, and tired of Montreal, he was eager to find a position elsewhere.

11

# 2 ◆ SPAIN

Fortunately for Bethune, a new attraction caught his interest. On 18 July 1936, General Francisco Franco of Spain led an armed uprising against the democratically elected national government in Madrid. This was the beginning of the Spanish Civil War, which pitted Nationalists against Republicans, or Loyalists. The Nationalists, led by Franco, included most members of the Spanish army, leaders of the Roman Catholic church in Spain, wealthy landowners and businessmen, and the Falange – the Spanish Fascist movement. Their Republican opponents comprised a handful of military officers, the navy and the air force, most factory and farm workers, the majority of intellectuals, and liberal and left-wing political parties.

From the outset, Bethune, siding with the Republican government, eagerly followed events in the conflict. Through July and August, despite his involvement in raising public awareness of his study group's medical proposals, Bethune focused his attention on the war in Spain. At the Hôpital du Sacré-Cœur, he openly revealed his support for the Republic, angering some of his co-workers and most certainly the Roman Catholic administrators of the institution.

By early September, Bethune had immersed himself in the unfolding events in Spain. Through newspaper and radio reports, he followed the virtually unimpeded progress of Franco's Army of the North as it advanced toward Madrid. About two weeks later, unlike many of his friends and most fellow members of the Communist Party, who lamented the increasingly bad news coming out of Spain but were unwilling to do anything, Bethune decided to take direct action. After trying in vain to borrow $200 from a friend for a trip to Spain, he offered his services to the Canadian Red Cross, which, as he then learned, did not intend to get involved in the Spanish conflict. Near the end of September, uncertain where to turn next, he read a front-page story in the *New Commonwealth*, a newspaper published in Toronto by the socialist CCF Party. The article stated that an organization had been set up to send a medical unit to Spain. Bethune immediately sent a telegram to Graham Spry, the newspaper's editor and author of the story, offering his services and indicating that he would drive to Toronto the next day to discuss the situation. When Bethune arrived at the newspaper office, Spry embarrassedly confessed that the organization did not exist. As a pacifist, he explained to Bethune, he was so appalled and angered by the apparent lack of public concern for the war that he had written the story in the hope of stirring up support for the real thing. Momentarily taken aback, Bethune was nonetheless impressed by Spry's sincerity. For his part, Spry was animated by Bethune's enthusiasm and suggested they put their heads together to consider how to make the unit a reality.

Within days, a group of liberals, socialists, and Communists set up the structure of an organization that they named the Committee to Aid Spanish Democracy (CASD). Their first step was to raise the funds necessary to buy medical supplies to send to Spain with Bethune. By mid-October Bethune had resigned from his position at the Hôpital du Sacré-Cœur and was concluding his affairs. As he was making his preparations, he continued to follow closely the worsening situation in Spain. On October 17, Franco's Army of the North launched an attack on Illescas, thirty kilometres southwest of Madrid, and the last Republican barrier between the Nationalist forces and the capital. Bethune now turned to poetry to express his feelings about these events. "Red Moon" was published nine months later in the magazine *Canadian Forum*.

And this same pallid moon tonight,
Which rides so quietly, clear and high,

13

The mirror of our pale and troubled gaze,
Raised to the cool Canadian sky.

Above the shattered Spanish mountain tops
Last night, rose low and wild and red,
Reflecting back from her illumined shield,
The blood bespattered faces of the dead,

To that pale disc we raise our clenchèd fists,
And to those nameless dead our vows renew,
"Comrades, who fought for freedom and the future world,
Who died for us, we will remember you."

*Canadian Forum* [Toronto], 17 July 1937

At a huge rally in Toronto on Wednesday, October 21, the CASD announced the formation of a medical mission led by Bethune. The focus of the meeting was a Spanish delegation made up of Isabel de Palencia, the Spanish ambassador to Sweden, Marcelino Domingo, a former minister of education, and Father Luis Sarasola, a Basque Roman Catholic priest. Sent by the Loyalist government to counter Nationalist propaganda, they arrived in Toronto to begin a North American speaking tour. Despite pouring rain, the arena was filled and hundreds were standing. After the Spaniards had spoken to round after round of applause, the chairman of the meeting announced that the CASD was about to send assistance to Spain. Then he turned, and referring to Bethune – who was sitting beside the Spaniards on the platform – as "Canada's ambassador to Spain," he motioned to him to come forward to speak.

"I stand here as a believer in democracy and as a humanitarian in the traditional role of the doctor to minister to those who need us," were the opening words of Bethune's brief speech, in which he stressed the need for medicines, which he hoped to be able to take with him. As he turned to return to his seat, Marcelino Domingo rose and clasped his arms around Bethune's shoulders in a typical Spanish embrace.

The CASD hoped that the success of the Toronto rally would be repeated in Montreal, where the Spanish delegation was scheduled to speak in the Mount Royal Arena on Friday night. However, trouble began

Saranac Lake 1928.
Photographer unknown.
(Roderick Stewart collection)

on Thursday morning when the Roman Catholic diocese of Montreal charged that Father Sarasola was an apostate whose opinions regarding the situation in Spain were contrary to those of the Pope and the bishops of Spain. Meanwhile, various right-wing elements accused the Spaniards of being Communists, and on Friday morning several hundred students from the Université de Montréal chanting "*À bas les communists!*" forced their way into City Hall. They warned elected officials that, unless they agreed to ban the rally, protesters would appear in much larger numbers at the Mount Royal Arena that evening with the intention of using violence to break it up. In response, the city council held a brief meeting in private; at the end of the meeting a councilor appeared to announce that they would instruct the chief of police to bar the doors of the Mount Royal Arena. To the cheers of the waiting students, the official concluded with: "We will not let Communism take root here."

Still hoping to introduce Bethune to at least a few Montrealers and to allow the Spanish delegation an opportunity to present their message, the

CASD rented a room in a downtown hotel for a meeting that began at 8:00 p.m. At 9:15, the manager knocked at the door and asked everyone to leave. He had received word that a mob of students armed with sticks was en route to the hotel determined to break up the meeting. While a group of men escorted the three Spaniards to their rooms in another hotel, the rest of the audience dispersed. Several newspaper reporters who had sat through the brief meeting approached Bethune for comment. Infuriated by what he characterized as the meek submission of city officials to Fascist threats and the overt restriction of free speech, Bethune angrily added, "The Montreal authorities are responsible for the deaths of 1,000 innocent women and children by their refusal to give a hearing to the Spanish delegates."

Early the following morning, carrying medical supplies including surgical instruments, blood transfusion equipment, anti-toxins, and serums, Bethune left for Quebec City, where he would begin his voyage to Spain. Waiting at dockside was a Canadian Press reporter, who stopped him as he was about to board the *Empress of Britain*. During a brief interview, the reporter commented that recent news reports from Spain suggested that Madrid might be under Franco's control before Bethune reached Spain. Bethune replied: "Whether or not Madrid falls before the invading forces, I will complete my mission."

Arriving in Paris on October 30, Bethune found a hotel room and made his way to the Spanish Embassy on avenue George V. Gaining an audience with the ambassador, Luis Araquistáin, he produced a letter identifying him as a representative of the CASD. Then he handed the ambassador an envelope containing $1,000 in American Express money orders. This sum, he explained, had been collected by the CASD for whatever purpose desired by Spanish medical authorities. In response, Araquistáin had a member of his staff prepare a *salvoconducto* (safe conduct) to allow Bethune to enter Spain.

Arriving in Madrid on Monday, November 2, he took a room in the Hotel Gran Via. Later that day he sent the following cable to the CASD:

Arrived safely flying from Toulouse, France to Alicante via Barcelona, to Madrid.

I brought surgical instruments, and vaccine. Spent $1000 on critical emergency for Oviedo. The Asturian miners there were in urgent need of anti-tetanic vaccine. For this emergency service, the Spanish embassy in Paris was very grateful.

Saw three aeroplane ambulances. Farman manufacture at Barcelona. Each of them had two stretchers; they are fine. These, I understand, were sent by the International Red Cross. I wish we had one.

Madrid is very optimistic. The enemy is six miles away, the streets of Madrid are crowded, half of the men are under arms, and many of the girls are armed.

All the shops are open. Food is plentiful and cheap. Only milk and meat have been rationed.

Thousands of posters are displayed. All are, of course, anti-Fascist. The upward, clenched fist is the salute of all four parties of the republic. There is much more socialist and anarchist propaganda than Communist.

Anti-aircraft sirens sound all day, but the crowds seem undisturbed and indifferent to danger.

I am meeting the International Red Cross and sanitary section of the government tomorrow (November 3).

New Commonwealth [Toronto], 21 November 1937

Taken in Paris by a studio
photographer in February 1937.
(Roderick Stewart collection)

Across the street from Bethune's hotel were the Hotel Florida and its popular bar, Perico Chicote, which attracted political correspondents, observers, and recently arrived foreign volunteers. On Tuesday afternoon, after having a drink, Bethune left the bar and walked back to his hotel. As he entered, he was stopped by a militiaman who had followed him from the bar. After listening briefly to the agitated and obviously unfriendly stranger, whose language he could not understand, Bethune turned to a hotel employee who had been watching the scene and who, fortunately for Bethune, spoke English. He told Bethune that the militiaman had heard Bethune use the word Fascist in the bar, and the well-tailored appearance of his shirt, tie, and jacket, along with his neatly trimmed moustache, made it apparent that he must be a Fascist spy. Barely able to suppress a derisive smile, Bethune quickly turned and walked up the stairs to his room.

Minutes later came the sound of voices and a sharp rap on his door. Opening it, Bethune was confronted by a police inspector, four guards, and the militiaman. When in response to a curt request for identification Bethune produced his passport and *salvoconducto*, the policeman closed the door and led away the guards and the clearly disappointed militiaman.

Less than a minute later, Bethune heard another knock and opened the door again. This time he encountered a tall, sandy-haired man in his early thirties who identified himself as Henning Sorensen. His appearance was no surprise: the CASD had informed Bethune that he would be meeting this man in Madrid. Shaking hands with Sorensen, he invited him in. Then, reaching into a suitcase, he pulled out a letter addressed to Sorensen that he had brought from Montreal.

Now the third act of the farce began. Once more there was a rapping at the door, and a somewhat bemused Bethune opened it to the now-familiar face of the police inspector. Ignoring Bethune, he strode quickly to Sorensen, snatched the letter from his hand, and ripped open the envelope. The salutation of "Darling" and the first couple of lines made it clear that this was a love letter. Quickly glancing at Sorensen's passport and *salvoconducto*, he somewhat sheepishly apologized and left the room.

Henning Sorensen. (Hazen Sise.
Library and Archives Canada
PA-172324)

Sorensen then assured Bethune that what had happened was not surprising. In the tense atmosphere of a Madrid under siege and full of strangers, the authorities were fearful of fifth columnists. Everyone was mistrustful, and no one was beyond suspicion. Disgusted at having been mistaken for a Fascist, Bethune decided to shave off his moustache and store away his ties.

Sorensen explained what had brought him to Spain. A multilingual Dane and naturalized Canadian, he had been led by his concern for the increasing misery caused by the economic depression to become interested in Marxist ideas. Believing that the outcome of the conflict in Spain would decide the fate of Communism and Fascism, Sorensen, like Bethune, resolved to make a personal contribution to the cause of the Left. On the eve of his departure for Spain at the end of September, Sorensen agreed to the request of Graham Spry, the *New Commonwealth* editor, to file articles on the war from Madrid. Three weeks later, on the day before Bethune sailed for Spain, the CASD cabled Sorensen in Madrid, asking him to meet Bethune when he arrived.

After only a few minutes of conversation, Bethune proposed that Sorensen give up his journalistic ambitions temporarily in order to act as his interpreter. In those few minutes, Bethune had made an impression on Sorensen, who liked Bethune's earnestness and could see that, like himself, he had come on a mission of mercy and was eager to help the Spanish people. Sorensen agreed to his request.

When Bethune explained his intention to offer his services as a surgeon to Spanish medical authorities, Sorensen suggested that, with a full-scale enemy assault expected at any moment, Bethune should consider going directly to the largest hospitals to speak to the chiefs of surgery. Beginning on Wednesday morning, they went first to Hospital Number One in the Palace Hotel, and then spent the next two days going from hospital to hospital. In almost every hospital, Bethune was told that there was little need for a chest surgeon, and in all of them – including the only one where he received a tentative offer – there was an unspoken but felt objection: Bethune could not speak Spanish.

Unable to find a place in a Madrid hospital, Bethune decided to offer himself for service in the International Brigades. However, although he impressed General Emilio Kléber of the XI International Brigade when they met at his headquarters in Cuidad Universitaria (University of Madrid), the chief of medical services, Dr. Fritz Fraenkel, refused to accept him. Bethune's quest to make a contribution to the Loyalist cause seemed to have come to an embarrassing end.

# 3 ◆ THE CANADIAN SERVICE

Deeply disappointed by the rejection of his services, Bethune turned to another idea. Learning that the International Brigades needed ambulances, he wired the CASD to send him $4,000 and left Madrid with Sorensen for Valencia, where he planned to buy an ambulance. During the early part of the train ride on the leg of their journey from Albacete, Bethune was absorbed in thought. Then suddenly he said, "Henning, I've got it!" He explained that he had been working out an idea that had been planted in his mind during their visits to hospitals. The wounded militiamen brought in on stretchers had reminded him of the Canadian soldiers he had carried from the trenches in France during the Great War. Wounded soldiers who had the misfortune to bleed copiously from their wounds before they were discovered went into circulatory shock and died, while those who reached casualty clearing stations before losing substantial amounts of blood often survived. Even some of those who had lost a great deal of blood could be saved if they were near a hospital with blood transfusion facilities. Unfortunately, as Bethune explained to Sorensen, not only were there few such hospitals, but the transfusion process required specially trained doctors in addition to donors whose blood type matched that of the recipient.

The process, which was called arm-to-arm or direct transfusion, took place with the wounded man and the donor lying on adjacent surgical tables. Blood extracted through a needle from a vein in the donor's arm flowed through a tube into a glass cannula inserted into a vein in the recipient's arm. In peacetime conditions this was a useful method, but in the hectic conditions of war it had serious limitations.

The most significant factor in the loss of life, Bethune pointed out, was the distance from the battlefield to transfusion facilities. This had given him an idea. Why not reverse the process and take the blood to the wounded? The blood would be extracted from donors in advance and stored in bottles that could be rushed on demand to hospitals or to casualty clearing stations near the front.

Bethune must have known of experiments conducted during the Great War in which whole blood had been used to transfuse wounded soldiers.

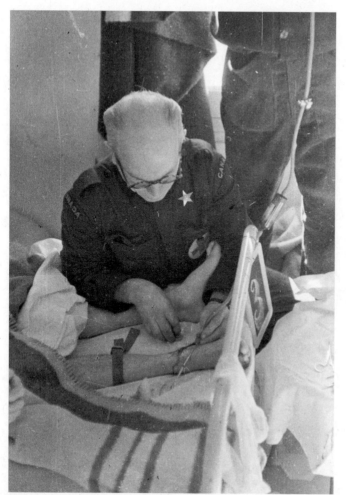

Performing a transfusion.
Photographer unknown.
(Library and Archives Canada
PA-116882)

Interestingly enough, among the tiny handful of military doctors who experimented with this practice, the first to make an analysis of the process and have his findings published in a scientific journal was Dr. Edward Archibald, Bethune's former chief at the Royal Victoria Hospital in Montreal. Commissioned as a Major in the Canadian Army Medical Corps, Archibald had carried out experiments with citrated blood – blood treated with sodium citrate to prevent coagulation – in casualty clearing stations during 1915 and 1916. It was from Archibald that Bethune had gained some knowledge of hematology and learned how to perform blood transfusions.

Ironically, a mobile blood transfusion service similar to the one he was now contemplating already existed in Spain. Set up by Dr. Frederic Durán i Jordà in Barcelona, it had begun to operate in September on the Aragon Front. However, in October, Franco made Madrid his main target, and conflict on the Aragon Front came to a virtual standstill. Few outside the Aragon Front, including officials of the SRI – Socorro Rojo Internacional (International Red Aid) – knew of Durán i Jordà and his work, and so Bethune was almost certainly unaware of it.

In Valencia, he was able to win approval to start a blood transfusion service only after many hours of discussion with the skeptical doctors who were among the SRI officials who listened to his plan. Final consent was gained only when Bethune assured them that his project would be financed entirely by Canadian money. He and Sorensen returned to Madrid and then left by plane for Paris on November 21. There they began to visit medical supply houses to purchase equipment. However, despite Sorensen's capable assistance as interpreter, Bethune became frustrated by the language barrier and decided to go to London.

Having lived in London for several years, Bethune knew exactly where to find the most recent papers on research in hematology, and he may have contacted doctors there who could provide him with advice. He set about finding a vehicle to be used to deliver bottled blood, and subsequently bought a new wood-panelled Ford station wagon. Because of the light tone of the wood, the Spaniards who later worked with Bethune called it *la rubia* (the blonde). After having the spare tire removed from the back of the vehicle and attached to the roof, he had the interior fitted

Hazen Sise. (Photographer unknown. Library and Archives Canada PA-172316)

out with a kerosene-operated fridge, a sterilizer, a gas-operated autoclave, a kerosene-run incubator and a water distiller. Enough space remained for a supply of bottles containing blood.

In London he also met Hazen Sise (1906–1974), a young Canadian from Montreal who was in the process of setting up a practice in architecture. Deeply concerned by events in Spain, and strongly impressed by Bethune and his proposed blood transfusion operation, Sise enthusiastically offered his services as a driver. On December 3, Sise, Sorensen, and Bethune left London for Folkstone and the ferry that would take them across the English Channel to the French port of Boulogne. Before leaving, Bethune sent the following cable to the CASD:

I spent a week in the trenches and only had the offer to go into a hospital as a surgeon. This I declined. I came to see they needed the organization of a blood transfusion service as only two or three of the big hospitals were providing these. Many men were dying from loss of blood as they lay on stretchers and in regimental aid posts.

I proposed to the government that the Canadian committee should undertake this work and finance it. They accepted with great enthusiasm. The Socorro Rojo Internacional have taken us under its wing. It is the most powerful organization of medical aid in Spain, looking after the wounded, the orphans and the widows ...

The completion of the work underway depends on Canadian antifascists. Much money is needed to complete the work, to pay for the ambulance, the apparatus, the hospital etc.

I appeal to all supporters of beleaguered Spanish democracy to rush funds to the Canadian committee so that it can be transmitted here without loss of time. The more quickly our work is actively commenced the more lives of heroic Spanish fighters will be saved.

I will use the latest Russian-American methods of collecting blood, storing it at suitable temperatures in vacuum bottles and transmitting it to any hospital needing it within 25 miles. Three girls on eight-hour shifts are on the telephones. A card index of 500 voluntary blood donors (all must have Wasserman tests) are some other essentials.

A regiment will turn up every day from which I will collect one or two gallons of blood. This I will store then rush out by a car which is equipped with special storage tanks and designed to prevent shock and jar to blood. I will administer the blood to the patients myself.

Special badges to donors are to be awarded, one star for each donation.

We need a lot of apparatus, sterilizers, sets of instruments, microscopes, etc. ...

*Daily Clarion* [Toronto], 4 December 1936

In Boulogne there was trouble at French Customs, where Bethune was told he had to pay duty on the station wagon and the medical supplies. Fearing that this might happen, Bethune had approached Vincent Massey, the Canadian High Commissioner in London, asking him for a letter of accreditation affirming that he was engaged in a humanitarian mission. After wiring the Department of External Affairs in Ottawa for instructions, Massey received a reply stating that because the CASD had connections with Communist Party members he must refuse Bethune's request. Bethune was enraged by the Canadian government's refusal to allow the free movement of medical materials designed to save lives in Spain, especially while Germany and Italy were openly sending men and weapons to Spain to destroy lives. When he returned to Canada he related this distressing incident in detail as often as he could.

After a brief stay in Paris, where they bought a few pieces of equipment that Bethune had been unable to find in London and visited the Spanish embassy to obtain a *salvoconducto* for Sise, they entered Spain at Portbou on December 8. Forced to stay overnight in Barcelona to allow repairs to be made to the Ford, they reached Valencia two days later. During two days of discussions with SRI officials, they learned that they would be able to set up the blood transfusion unit at the SRI headquarters in Madrid.

On Monday, December 14, they moved into their quarters at 36 Príncipe de Vergara in the Salamanca district on the east side of the city, several blocks north of the Parque del Buen Retiro. Inhabited by middle- and upper-middle class Madrileños, Salamanca had so far been spared from the daily aerial and artillery bombardment that had begun on November 16. Early Saturday morning, in response to newspaper and radio appeals, a long line of potential donors lined the street below the apartment building, waiting for the doors to open. The Instituto canadiense de transfusión de sangre, a name chosen by Bethune, began to

Bethune and Sorensen, en route to Spain, in front of the Hotel du Quai Voltaire in Paris, December 1936. (Hazen Sise. Library and Archives Canada PA-116885)

operate. On December 17, Bethune wrote his first extended report to Benjamin Spence, chairman of the CASD in Toronto.

Dear Ben:

This is really the first time since my arrival in this country that I can give you definite news and detailed information.

I am glad to say that we are now completely organized and settled in for work. As I wrote you before (I hope you received my letter) unless we were able to offer the Government some definite proposal and concrete scheme our efforts would peter out – by this I mean I would simply go into a hospital as a surgeon and that would be the end of the "Canadian Unit." Now it seemed better to emulate England and Scotland and establish ourselves as a definite entity. England has the "English Hospital," Scotland has the "Scottish Ambulance."

So with this in mind and after making several blind starts (such as the two days we spent at the front with the International Brigade) Sorensen and I left for Paris to collect apparatus and [a] car.

No cars are for sale in Spain. I had in mind a Ford station car, as a compromise between a truck and a car. It must carry about $1^1/_2$ tons of cargo, could be used as an ambulance if needed for such and yet it would be handy enough to transport 4 people in comparative comfort.

I couldn't buy this car in Paris. I had to go to London. Here I was able to pick one up for one hundred and seventy five pounds sterling and with alterations such as luggage rack on top, built in boxes etc. [It] made a good type of transportation for our purpose so I bought complete equipment for a mobile blood transfusion service.

The idea of mobility was always kept in mind so such apparatus as refrigerators, autoclave, incubators, etc. all were purchased to run by gasoline or kerosene and to be independent of electrical power.

The refrigerator is Electrolux run by kerosene and very efficient. The auto clave (for sterilization of solutions, bottles, etc.) is run by gasoline, the incubator by kerosene and the distilled water still by kerosene.

So our four major pieces of apparatus run to about one ton in weight (the auto clave weighs about 450 lbs itself). They take up the major part of the interior.

The Ford station wagon loaded with equipment in Paris, December 1936.
(Hazen Sise. Roderick Stewart collection)

Then in addition we have 175 pieces of glassware of all varieties and kinds
– vacuum bottles, blood flasks, drip bottles, containers etc. We have 3 complete direct blood transfusion sets of the latest English model (Froud syringe)
microscope haemocytometers, complete set of chest instruments, 2000 sets
of type 2 and 3 blood serum for testing blood groups, hurricane lamps, gas
masks etc.

In all, our equipment consists of 1,375 separate pieces. We have enough
chemicals to make up solutions for intravenous injections of physiological
serums, glucose and sodium citrate to last us for three months, I estimate.

These chemicals are packed in water-tight tin cases and each is weighed
out separately so that by adding each package to a given amount of distilled
water the proper strength of solution is obtained.

Now we are installed in a 15 room flat formerly occupied by a German
diplomat (Fascist, now in Berlin), very magnificent and palatial, at the above
address. Just above us are the S.R.I. (Socorro Rojo Internacional) head offices.
We are working under their protection. They are the best organized and most
powerful health organization in Spain and much superior to the International Red Cross (this organization is very suspiciously Fascist between you
and I) or the weak Spanish Red Cross.

The S.R.I. was formed before the revolution to care for the political prisoners and their families who suffered Fascist oppression and since the revolution has gradually taken over the majority of the sanitary services of the

country. Their work in the rescue of orphans and evacuation of abandoned areas is tremendous. They run about 1,000 orphanages, camps, hospitals, crèches etc. in Spain. All their leaders are party people – as everywhere in Spain the people who lead the major services are Communists – they do the hard and dirty work.

Now as to our organization. Through the press and daily over the local radio we broadcast appeals for blood donors. As a result we have thousands of volunteers and are busy grouping them and card indexing them. We have now 800 and in a few days will have over 1,000. There are about 56 hospitals in the City. We have surveyed the entire situation and have a list of them containing the information as to size, capacity, addresses, under what organization, telephone, chief surgeon, type of service etc. A large map of the City (4 x 5 ft.) in our office (the former library, the walls entirely lined by 8,000 books, gold brocade curtains and Aubusson carpets!) gives at once the route to the hospitals.

We collect the blood every day from a selected group of donors types I, II, III, IV. We are running about 1 gallon daily just now. This is stored in our refrigerator. On call from the hospital the blood flasks are transferred to heated vacuum bottles and carried in knapsacks with additional bottles, warm physiological serum and glucose solution plus a complete sterilized tin box containing:

Towel
Forceps
knife
syringe
catgut

We have 15 complete group testing serum sets.

So on arrival we're ready to start work at once. We go to the man and decide what he needs – either blood or physiological serum, or glucose or a combination of these. If blood is needed on account of acute exsanguination we "group" him at once with our serum. This is done by a prick of the finger, a glass stick and serum and takes 2 minutes, then after grouping we give him the blood of the type needed (type I, II, III, or IV).

If in doubt we can always give IV as this is called the "Universal" donor. We are not sure how long the citrated blood will keep good in our refrigerators but we are experimenting and hope for several weeks.

*Above*
Bethune showing a donor
a refrigerator containing
bottled blood in the quarters
of the Instituto canadiense.
(Geza Kárpáthi. National
Film Board of Canada)

*Left*
Operating room in the
bombed-out district of
Cuatro Caminos.
(Hazen Sise. Roderick
Stewart collection)

We have plans to branch out and give the service up in the Guadarrama Mountains up to a distance of 100 miles from the City later and might need another car but this won't be for several months yet.

Now as to personnel – I, myself am of course director, Henning Sorensen is Liaison officer, Hazen Sise is driver and general utility man (he is a Canadian, the son of Paul Sise, president of the Northern Electric Co. of Montreal, a talented young architect) then we have 2 Spanish medical students, a Spanish Biologist and Mrs. Celia Greenspan of New York (wife of M. Greenspan the journalist) as technician. We have a staff of 4 servants, a cook, 2 maids and [a] laundry man, also a military armed guard for our door. We are all well and happy.

About one quarter of the City is badly damaged and abandoned except by troops. 300,000 people, mostly women, children and aged have been evacuated. Between 7–8 thousand civilians have been killed by bombardment in the last month and many more thousand wounded.

Morale is excellent. Madrid won't fall but will be the tomb of Fascism!

Junker machines (3 motor bombers) came over yesterday at 6 p.m. accompanied by 24 pursuit planes; they dropped several tons of bombs. I took some photos of a hit hospital in the afternoon. Their 100 and 250 kilo bombs make an awful mess!

Just now there is a lull but Franco has declared he will not leave one stone standing in Madrid. Well let him try.

The water is still good. No epidemics have broken out as yet. The electric light is on but the gas is very low and reserved for hospitals. Coal is practically gone and meat is scarce, no milk, butter, sugar but plenty of vegetables and fruit (oranges and apples).

Well, we are here "for the duration" as we used to say in 1914. I can only say how grateful I am for the wonderful backing of the committee and the people of Canada.

The $1,800.00 I came over with – $1,000.00 went to the Oviedo Miners for Anti Tetanus Serum and the $800.00 was spent in travelling and living expenses for Sorensen and myself in Spain and back to London (incidentally I would have been lost in these early days without his Spanish and French). The $3,000.00 received in Paris and the additional $4,000.00 in London went into the car and equipment ($1,200.00 in duty (refundable)) leaving a balance of cash in hand now sufficient to keep the unit in this country under

31

present conditions for 3 months more. Of this cash on hand, $2,000.00 is in American Express orders and the balance ($500.00) in Spanish Pesetas and the dollar is fixed by the Government at 12 pesetas or roughly 9 cents. Prices are spiked and there is no inflation.

I am enclosing a photo but will send you a better one next week. This was taken on our arrival last week. I enclose also samples of our stationery. A Medal is being struck for our donors with a Star for each donation. Will send you next week a photo and a badge also. This letter is going out with a member of the Scottish Ambulance which is returning to Scotland to be re-organized.

Best of luck to everybody and a Merry Christmas.
Your comrade
Norman Bethune

P.S. This unit is causing considerable interest among the Foreign Press but I am keeping back the story until next week, when I have informed the Press Censor (an Austrian Comrade – !) it may be released as you will probably hear about it before this letter reaches you.

N.B.

> Research file for documentary film *Bethune* (1964)
> National Film Board Library, Montreal

Bethune now decided it was time to take a short holiday in which he and his comrades could combine duty with pleasure by conducting a brief inspection of hospitals in the Guadarramas. Before leaving Madrid, he completed two propaganda tasks. The first was to make a Christmas Eve radio broadcast that was beamed to North American listeners over the Madrid shortwave station EAQ. The following is the text:

Comrades of Spain: I, and my comrades of the Canadian Blood Transfusion Service have the honour to be in Spain as the representatives of the Canadian Committee to Aid Spanish Democracy.

This committee, with headquarters in Toronto, Canada, is formed of workers and intellectuals, of liberals and socialists and Communists. We, the United Front of Canada, join hands with the United States of Spain – The International Anti-Fascists of the old and new worlds.

When we first came to Spain, two months ago, you used to talk to us about your war, your revolution, but now you are beginning to speak about our war, Spain's war, Canada's war, England's war, the war of the workers of the world. And that is a good sign. It is a sign that the causes and consequences of our struggle are deeper and more-far reaching than the boundaries of the Pyrenees, across the English Channel, across the Atlantic and include the world.

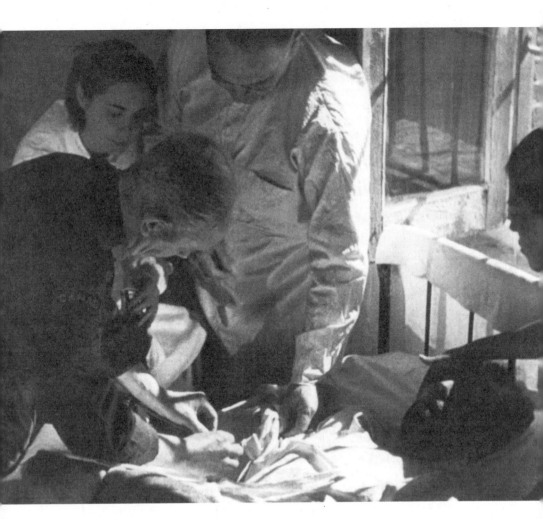

Transfusion. (Photographer unknown. Roderick Stewart collection)

The revolution of the workers against the economic, religious and intellectual slavery happened to have occurred this year in Spain. It might just as well have happened in a dozen other countries but that you had the courage, the dignity and the audacity to face your problems with more open eyes, firmer lips and stouter hearts than the workers of the rest of the world.

What Spain does today, what you Spaniards do tomorrow, will decide the future of the world for the next 100 years. If you are defeated the world will fall back into the new dark ages of Fascism – if you are successful, as we are confident you will be successful, we will go forward into the glories of the new golden age of economic and political democracy.

Remember we Canadian workers are with you. We have come here as into the opening battle of the world revolution. Your fight is our fight. Your victory is our victory. Ask us how we can help you. You will find us ready to respond. Salud.

"Canada Greets Spain"
*This is Station EAQ Madrid*
Osler Library of the History of Medicine, McGill University
Norman Bethune Collection P156, accession 445B, folder 3

His other task was to send the following cable to the CASD and urge them to have it published. Entitled "A Letter to All Canadian Doctors," it was an invitation to the members of his profession in Canada to volunteer to join him in Spain.

Dear Doctor:
The Canadian Committee to Aid Spanish Democracy is sending me as a bearer of medical supplies, blood-transfusion equipment and serums to the Spanish, and to head a distinctively Canadian Medical unit to work in close co-operation with similar missions from other countries, and in cordial relations with the Spanish Government military authorities.

I am undertaking this work as a doctor and a humanitarian. In view of the terrible suffering which the Spanish democratic workers are undergoing in their heroic fight against the Rebel Fascist forces, we doctors cannot stand aside and view the present tragic situation of millions of desperate people without physicians and adequate medical aid, with the detachment of any political opinion.

With a Republican unit in the Guadarrama Mountains, Christmas 1936. Sise is seated at Bethune's right. (Henning Sorensen. Roderick Stewart collection)

To come to the relief of human suffering is the historic and traditional role of the medical profession. Our duty is plain and inescapable. There are at present hospital and ambulance units in Spain from England, Scotland, France and Scandinavian countries. Canada should be and must be represented. It will be.

May I urge you to join with me in this non-political humanitarian effort? Will you please communicate with the Canadian Committee to Aid Spanish Democracy, 304 Manning Chambers, N.W. corner Queen and Bay Streets, Toronto, regarding any assistance you feel you can render.

Yours very truly,
Norman Bethune

*New Commonwealth* [Toronto], 26 December 1936

At one of the hospitals they inspected in the Guadarramas, Bethune and his companions were invited by an officer to visit a fortified outpost at the front. They went in an armoured car high into the mountains to an abandoned sanatorium where an alpine battalion was stationed. The commandant and some of the other soldiers, all of them in their twenties, had brought their wives to the post. Warmly receiving the Canadians, the commandant invited them to join in holiday celebrations. Although snow covered the ground, it was a mild day; the afternoon sun was bright as a table and chairs were set up, the women brought out food and wine, and a soldier produced a guitar and started to play. After lunch their hosts took them back to the hospital; on Christmas Day they guided them to the headquarters of a nearby ski battalion. Borrowing equipment from the Spaniards, Bethune, Sise, and Sorensen skied over several hills. From the outpost they gazed down on El Escorial, the magnificent palace built by Carlos V, which was now being used as a hospital. Later that afternoon they drove down to visit it.

Skiing in the Guadarramas, Christmas 1936.
(Hazen Sise. Library and Archives Canada PA-117449)

# 4 ◆ THE VOICE OF PROTEST

Inspired by what he regarded as the "good proletarian spirit" of the alpine battalion, and by the calibre of personnel and efficiency of performance he had noted in the hospitals he had inspected, Bethune truly believed that he was witnessing the dawn of a new world in Spain. His enthusiasm was reflected in his second radio broadcast, made two days after his return from the Guadarramas on December 29.

It gives me great pleasure to describe my personal observations regarding the care of the sick and wounded in Madrid. I believe I am competent to do so on account of my experience not only as a doctor who served [in] the Great War 1914–1918 but as one who held, up to the time of his arrival in Spain, the post of chief of Service, Department of Thoracic Surgery and Bronchoscopy, Sacré Coeur Hospital, Montreal, Canada. So what I will say will be based on personal observations.

There are in Madrid today 57 hospitals with a total of over ten thousand beds. They range from huge Military Hospitals, such as the Palace Hotel, each with over a thousand beds, entirely confined to wounded cases, down to small 50-bed special hospitals for cancer, etc. Not only are the usual sicknesses of the civil population being carefully taken care of but the thousands of wounded are receiving expert care and attention.

As an example of this, come with me to a large military hospital such as the Palace Hotel. Its operating room, in its great dining room, with tremendous crystal chandeliers and glittering gold mirrors, has eight tables, side by side, each staffed by two doctors, an anaesthetist and nurse. Here some of the most famous surgeons of Spain, the equal, to say the least of any country in the world, are at work, each on his own specialty.

This first one is a famous brain surgeon who is now exploring a wound of the head. He once received $5000 for a similar operation in private practice, now he does it gladly for his $1.00 a day.

Next to him a great abdominal surgeon is sewing up carefully multiple perforations of the intestine of a soldier shot through the abdomen. Notice his movements. They are as quick, as expert, as careful, as those which made him an international figure in his profession. This is his 20th operation today. He is tired and weary but his love of his countrymen, his pride in his art is as high as ever.

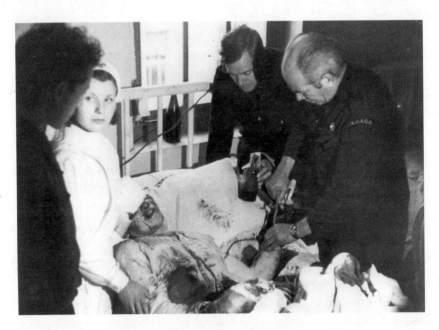

With Sorensen, performing a transfusion near Guadalajara, March 1937. (Geza Kárpáthi. Library and Archives Canada c-067451)

On the next table is a German soldier (an anti-fascist) shot through the thigh with a dum-dum bullet – the exit of its passage is large enough to hold one's clenched fist. He must have anti-tetanus serum and a blood transfusion before he leaves the table.

Here is another – a Pole – shot through the shoulder and the bullet has not yet appeared. There is no guess work. Before he comes on the table the X-ray shows exactly where the bullet may be successfully extracted.

Now all this is very spectacular. But what is happening above in the wards. Here they lie – row on row – Spaniards, English, German, Italians, French, Belgium, Scotch, Irish, American. The wounded soldiers of the greatest Anti-Fascist army the world has yet seen. They represent the United Front of International Anti-Fascism. They have fought this war for you and for me. They need your help.

"How?" you ask. First they need nurses who can speak their own language. It is more important that a wounded man should be nursed by a woman who can speak his own language than be operated on by a surgeon who many understand nothing more than the technical problem involved. Then they need the food of the home-land prepared by these hands who nurse them.

The delights of scrambled eggs on toast with a cup of English tea would be like a gift from heaven to stomachs not yet attuned to olive oil and Spanish beans. So I see the need for an International Nursing Corps of French, German and English nurses; principally to nurse the sick and wounded of the heroes of the International Brigade.

Now this is what is needed in Spain:

More physicians who speak French or German, if not Spanish.

More brain surgeons, on account of the high proportion of the head injuries owing to lack of proper protection of the skull by steel helmets. The Chief Surgeon of one of the fronts told me on Christmas Day that 70 percent of head wounds could have been prevented by the use of steel helmets – but he added bitterly – "France and England would not let us buy steel helmets to save our lives against German and Italian bullets."

More foreign nurses to be attached to hospitals treating the wounded from the International Brigade.

A convalescent home and club for the German, French, English, Italian and Polish members of the International Brigade. Think of being in a country, say like these Englishmen in a German Battalion, of being wounded and in a hospital and being operated on and nursed by those who could not speak a single word of English – of being discharged and wandering about Madrid lonely, discouraged and sad.

Now who in England will provide these. Here is a project to make happier the lives of some of the finest of young British manhood I have ever had the pleasure to meet. These young men, some of them not yet 20 but most between 20 and 30, are fighting for ideals as pure, as strongly felt, as [the ideals that] animated their Anglo-Saxon Ancestors in the Wars of the Crusades. And they are fighting to save this land, this pleasant land of Spain, from the grasps of the Fascist infidel – who denies by word and action belief in the virtue of mankind, his ability to govern himself, freed from political dictatorship and economic oppression.

We need more ambulances. More splints. More X-ray films.

We would also be glad to hear from those who are listening in nightly as we are not sure of the number of our audience. Will you drop me a line?

And now we wish you a Happy New Year.

We are happy here too because we know that 1937 will see the International Fascists driven from this land for ever. Spain will be free and the second great fight against the threat of the New Dark Ages of Fascism will be defeated. All men of good will should not only earnestly desire but must purposefully act towards that end. SALUD.

"Practical International Comradeship"
*This is Station EAQ Madrid, Spain*
Osler Library of the History of Medicine, McGill University
Norman Bethune Collection P156, accession 445B, folder 3

The unit was now beginning to collect blood, calling on donors who had registered before Christmas. After receiving assurance from the donor that he or she had fasted (so that the blood collected would not be contaminated with fat), they extracted 500 cc of blood. It flowed into a bottle to which was added a small amount of sodium citrate. On a label fixed to the bottle were recorded the type of blood, the donor's name, and the date of the extraction. The blood was then refrigerated at between two and four degrees Celsius. At first, donors received a voucher for a small amount of

With Vera Elkan, likely in January 1937. (Hazen Sise. Library and Archives
Canada PA-117423)

food, but later each was given a tin of bully beef. In addition, a bottle of
brandy was always present to offer a shot to each donor.

During those last few days of December, Bethune found time to write
another address, which was broadcast on New Year's Day, 1937.

There has been heavy fighting today. As we were working at our job in the
hospitals, the staccato tick-tack-tack of machine guns came through the
windows, as if they were firing at the end of the street, so clear is this cold
Spanish winter air. In truth, they were nearly a mile distant.

The burst of field gun-fire has been almost continuous[,] reminding your
commentator of the barrages on the Western Front in 1915. To these dangers
are added the attacks of fascist bombers, attended by their fighting escort.

In today's attack, by 15 German and Italian bombers, five of the [escort] fighters attacked one solitary Spanish government pursuit plane. They set him on fire, but as he fell, overcome in the unequal contest, he charged full-out, head-on into one of Franco's planes. They fell together, in flames, crashing into a vine-covered hill one hundred yards apart. Both pilots were killed instantly.

As I happened to be at a clearing station hospital close by, we walked across the fields to inspect the wreckage. I took from the fascist machine the plate off its engine and have it in front of me as I speak. The pilot was a young German military pilot.

Now within sight of these planes in the cemetery of the International Brigade here row on row lie the bodies of those men who died as Anti-Fascists to save Spain from the fate of their own countries. They – these workers, students and intellectuals, who so dedicated their young lives in the cause of Spanish Democracy, are from every country in Europe. They are from Italy, Germany, France, England, Scotland, Ireland, Poland, Czechoslovakia and Austria.

These young men volunteered fully and they travelled, many in disguise, thousands of miles from their native lands, working their way out secretly

Bethune examining the nameplate
of a downed German plane.
(Hazen Sise. Library and Archives
Canada PA-116886)

to escape the police terrorism. They left their wives and families and in the pride of their young strength and fine political convictions, died under this old Spanish sun, on the bare hills, among the vines and olive trees of this beautiful land surrounded by people of whom not more than a handful could speak their own language, facing over-whelming odds of trained mercenary professional troops. Against a military machine dominated by German and Italian Staff Officers, fighting with rifles, some of them dating before the so-called Great War of 1914, against modern German and Italian machine guns, without steel helmets or proper clothing.

From German cities, from Italian towns, from French villages, English farms, Scottish highlands and American plains, these serious, calm-eyed, earnest workmen and intellectuals and students came, thinking not of their personal comfort or safety, fighting not for money (their pay was 10 pesetas – about 50¢ a day) fighting not for King or Country, not at the frantic urging of selfish bank barons or masters of finance, who saw their profits in danger, but fighting and dying for an ideal of human freedom. From that same high motivation spoken of so many centuries ago – "Greater love hath no man than this that he should lay down his life for his friend." And that "friend" was not only the Spanish worker groaning under the cruel heel and iron fist of monopoly capitalism and religious bigotry, but the workers of the world suffering under these same masters in other countries, in your country and in mine

And here they lie, quietly and still. And see what is written above their heads: "Volunteers of the International Brigade" – "Who died as heroes for the liberty of the Spanish people and the happiness and progress of human-ity." Above each grave is written his name, his nationality and the date of his death.

"They Made the Supreme Sacrifice"
*This is Station EAQ Madrid, Spain*
Osler Library of the History of Medicine, McGill University
Norman Bethune Collection P156, accession 445B, folder 3

As Bethune was making the broadcast, a new Nationalist offensive aimed at cutting Madrid's line of communication to the north was already in progress. Although the unit now became busily involved in its first blood-supply operations for hospitals receiving the wounded, on January

Members of the Instituto canadiense with members of the International Brigades. (Photographer unknown. Roderick Stewart collection)

2 Bethune was able to make a broadcast in which he described the conditions and atmosphere of Madrid during the continuing siege.

Madrid is, paradoxically enough, the most peaceful city in Europe. It is a city at equilibrium within itself, a city without the intense class antagonisms and discords that are called disorder in any other city. That is due to its homogeneous society – the workers, the small shop-keepers and the petit-bourgeois all molded into one class with one idea – winning the war against the Fascist aggressor.

So, as in a family or clan in which there is internal peace although the family or clan may be fighting against its external enemies. No police are needed to maintain the law. Every member, every citizen, is under the strict necessity of order – self-imposed and conscious.

Private property is respected – confiscated property belonging to the people at large, is equally respected. On large magnificent mansions, which

44

once belonged to the late so-called nobility, one may see signs such as these: "Citizens, this property belongs to you, respect it." Note the wording of the sign – not "Belongs to the State" – the State as an institution superior to and above the people, but – "belongs to you" – belongs to me. So, if you or I damage it, we are damaging our own property.

There is absolutely no looting. This is clear from one manifest fact – the things which are looted in a war are first of all articles of necessity such as clothing and food. Later come the luxuries – jewels, fur coats, etc. Now the people of Madrid are wearing the same clothes as they wore before the rebellion in spite of the large quantities of fine clothes left by fleeing Fascists and members of the so-called upper classes.

Buying of necessities and clothing is brisk in the shops. I was in a large departmental store today and saw a woman of the so-called middle classes buy a tricycle for her boy of 10 and a large doll for her daughter of 5.

We were heavily bombed from the air today about 12 noon. Twelve huge Italian tri-motored bombers came over the city and bombed not positions of military importance, but a poor quarter of the city – called Cuatro Caminos. This is a district some miles behind the front line, inhabited by the poorest people living in one or two storey mud and brick dwellings. The massacred victims were mainly women, children and old people.

Standing in a doorway as these huge machines flew slowly overhead, each one heavily loaded with bombs, I glanced up and down the streets. People hurried to "refugios"; a hush fell over the city – it was a hunted animal crouched down in the grass, quiet and apprehensive. There is no escape, so be still. Then in the dead silence of the streets the songs of birds came startlingly clear in the bright winter air.

What is the object of these bombings of lowly civilian habitations? Is it to produce panic in the city? Because, if so, it is a completely cruel, useless and wanton endeavour. These people cannot be terrified. They are being treated by the Fascists as if they were soldiers bearing offensive arms. This is murder of defenseless civilians.

No one can realize what utter helplessness one feels when these huge death-ships are overhead. It is practically useless to go into a building – even a ten-storey building. The bombs tear through the roof, through every floor in the building and explode in the basement bringing down concrete buildings as if they were made of matchwood.

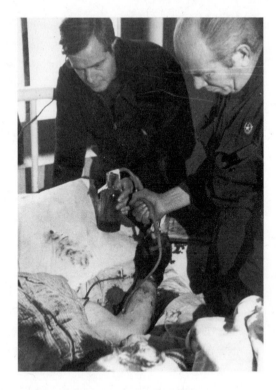

With Sorenson, giving a
transfusion to a wounded soldier.
(Geza Kárpáthi. Library and
Archives Canada e007151988)

It is not much safer to be in the basement of the lower floors, than in the upper stories. One takes shelter in doorways to be out of the way of falling masonry, huge pieces of facade and stone work. If the building you happen to be in is hit, you will be killed or wounded. If it is not hit, you will not be killed or wounded. One place is really as good as another.

After the bombs fall – and you can see them falling like great black pears – there is a thunderous roar. Clouds of dust and explosive fumes fill the air, whole sides of houses fall into the street. From heaps of huddled clothes on the cobblestones blood begins to flow – these were once live women and children.

Many are buried alive in the ruins. One hears their cries – they cannot be reached. Burst water and gas mains add to the danger. Ambulances arrive. The blackened and crumpled bodies of the still-alive are carried away.

Now observe the faces of, not the dead, but those who still live. Because it is the wished-for effect on them which is the motive for these massacres, not just the killing of a few hundred innocent civilians and the destruction of property, but the terrorizing of hundreds of thousands who escaped this death. They stand and watch or work themselves at the rescue. Their lips are set and cold. They don't shout or gesticulate. They look at each other sorrowfully, and when they talk of the fascist assassins, their faces express fortitude, dignity and contempt.

These people have endured from the arrogance of wealth, the greed of the church, the poverty and oppression of centuries. This is just one more blow, one more lash of the whip. They have stood these blows, these lashes before and they will stand them to the end. They cannot be shaken.

"Madrid! Peaceful Amid War"
*This is Station EAQ Madrid, Spain*
Osler Library of the History of Medicine, McGill University
Norman Bethune Collection P156, accession 445B, folder 3

During this time, Bethune turned to poetry to express his emotional reaction to the violence of the war suffered by the people in Cuatro Caminos, a working-class sector of the city. Unlike Salamanca, the sector where most affluent Madrileños lived and that, therefore, was not a target for German and Italian bombers, Cuatro Caminos was systematically and heavily attacked from the air. Reacting in bitter anger, Bethune wrote the following poem.

Bethune in the Instituto canadiense uniform. (Hazen Sise. Roderick Stewart collection)

I come from Cuatro Caminos,
From Cuatro Caminos I come,
My eyes are overflowing,
And clouded with blood.
The blood of a little fair one,
Whom I saw destroyed on the ground;
The blood of a young woman,
The blood of an old man, a very old man,
The blood of many people, of many
Trusting, helpless,
Fallen under the bombs
Of the pirates of the air.
I come from Cuatro Caminos,
From Cuatro Caminos I come,
My ears are deaf
With blasphemies and wailings,
Ay Little One, Little One;
What hast thou done to these dogs
That they have dashed thee in pieces
On the stones of the grounds?
Ay, ay, ay, Mother, my Mother;
Why have they killed the old grandfather?
Because they are wolf's cubs,
Cubs of a man-eating wolf.
Because the blood that runs in their veins
Is blood of brothel and mud
Because in their regiment
They were born fatherless
A "curse on God" rends the air
Towards the infamy of Heaven.

> Research file for documentary film *Bethune* (1964)
> National Film Board Library, Montreal

On January 5, in what would be his final radio broadcast, Bethune described what he believed to be the ideological source of the will of the people of Madrid to endure the Nationalist siege.

This is an appeal, if such an appeal is necessary to any scientific or common-sense person, especially to psychologists and those interested in contemporaneous psychological problems, such as war, to come to Madrid and see their theories of "Masses," of "mobs," put to the test of reality.

These fashionable theories, too many of those formulated in laboratories or in armchairs or from observation of lower animals, have been accepted by the laity as truths beyond the necessity of proof. But, if some of these theories of the "mass men," the "mass women," be subjected to the scrutiny of reality, there is a possibility of a wide divergence between theory and scientific observation.

Now what I am driving towards is this: Today the fashionable explanations of the individual are in terms introduced by Freud or Adler – in terms of sexual domination or the will-to-power. "The instinct of the herd," as Trotter calls it, the motives which animate the mass or the nation, as a people at war, is defined principally in terms of the defence of property. Now this is true of a capitalistic war, but it is not true of this war.

I remember the so-called Great War of 1914–1918 and compare to myself, the emotions of the people of say London or Paris then to those of the people of Madrid today. In the former case, in the early days, there was a high-pitched almost hysterical feeling in the air, engendered by propaganda, a hatred of the Germans as beasts of prey, against their aggression towards a peaceful people, of their ruthlessness toward the innocent bystander – Belgium. The true issues at stake were never clarified. The truth in full was never told.

Such old methods of propaganda are not seen now in these parts of Spain held by the government. The appeal now is deeper, more profound, more truthful. Franco and his mercenary troops, Moors, Foreign Legionaires, Germans and Italians, are not only depicted as ruthless, immoral and vicious, but it is explained why they are ruthless, immoral and vicious. They are shown as aggressors, against the most elementary rights of man.

It seems to me that such an appeal was seldom or never made – at least from our side, in the last war. And this simplification in propaganda of war motives – from Franco's side, the necessity of keeping the worker in subjection and on our side, the determination to end economic, religious and intellectual slavery, gives to these people in Madrid tremendous unity and power that must be seen to be believed.

It gives this war the aspect of a holy war, a religious war – and by that I mean the union of common sense rationalism with profound subconscious, only partly articulated instincts, one of these instincts is that a man should be – to call himself a man – free from dictatorship and from domination by his fellow man. The Spaniard is not fighting for "King and Country"; he is fighting for his rights as a man. He is fighting for Spain of course because this is his beloved land, but for more than that.

The people of Madrid may be seen as [a] unified and consolidated mass of both emotional and intellectual forces. This gives them strength and endurance. Against the daily bombardment of German and Italian airplanes, against hunger and cold. Nothing less than this unification of the intellect and the emotions could produce such profound belief in this rightness of their fight against the fascist aggressor. And this is why the people of Spain are fighting so courageously, so fiercely, against International Fascism.

Here are no imported ideologies, no Moscow gold, no third International dictatorship, and their motives in the struggle are indigenous to themselves. They arise from the local conditions of economics and religious oppression and by reason of their indigenous source they possess a gratifying growth and strength which makes their success assured.

"Wars Contrasted! 1914–1918 and 1936–37"
*This is Station EAQ Madrid, Spain*
Osler Library of the History of Medicine, McGill University
Norman Bethune Collection P156, accession 445B, folder 3

Finally, in response to a cabled request from the CASD that Bethune send more information on his activities and those of the unit, he wrote the following letter on January 11, his second to Benjamin Spence in Toronto.

Dear Ben:
We have had a very hectic ten days as you may know and I haven't really had the time to sit down and write you a letter but as an Englishman is leaving today for Paris I felt I should take advantage of this and let you know the news.

Frank Pitcairn – author of "A Reporter in Spain," promised to write an article on our unit for the "Daily Worker" of London whose correspondent he

The Renault ambulance in the Guadarramas, spring 1937. (Hazen Sise. Roderick Stewart collection)·

is. But as he hasn't turned up today – he stays with us – I expect he has left for another front.

Professor J.B.S. Haldane, who stayed with us for two weeks, has returned to London and has promised to send "The Clarion" an article on us. I think this would be better than one I might write myself.

As you know we have withstood the heaviest attack and the most serious effort of the Fascists to take the City since the first and second weeks of November. Their losses have been terrific – at least 5,000 (our papers say 10,000) Germans have been killed and Franco has taken the Moors away from Madrid and replaced them with fresh German troops. They thought they had a walk-over and advanced in exactly the same massed formation as they did in 1914–1915 in France. Our machine guns simply mowed them down. Our losses were 1 to 5 of theirs.

The International Brigade has suffered badly of course as they are [not] shock troops but large re-inforcements of French, German, English, Polish, Austrian and Italians – with some Americans and Canadians ... arriving.

We have been having 2 & 4 raids a day for 2 weeks now and many thousands of non-combatants, women and children, have been killed. I was in the Telephonic Building the other day when it was shelled. However, it is very modern and strongly built. No great damage was done – a handful of people were killed only.

You simply can't get these people to take shelter during shelling and bombing!

Our night work is very eerie! We get a phone call for blood. Snatch up our packed bag, take 2 bottles (each 500 c.c.) – one of group IV and one of group II blood – out of the refrigerator and with our armed guard off we go through the absolutely pitch dark streets and the guns and machine guns and rifle shots sound like as if they were in the next block, although they are really half a mile away. Without lights we drive, stop at the hospital and with a search light in our hands find our way into the cellar principally. All the operating rooms in the hospitals have been moved into the basement to avoid falling shrapnel, bricks and stones coming through the operating room ceiling.

Our bag contains a completely sterilized box of instruments, towels etc. so we can start work at once. The man is lying most frequently on a stretcher so we kneel down beside him, prick the finger and on a slide put 1 drop each of Serum type II and type III. If his red blood cells are agglutinated by II and not by III – he is a type III. If agglutinated by II he is a III, if by both he is a type I, if neither, he is a group IV.

So now we know what blood he can take safely. If I, III or IV he gets our bottle of blood group IV (the universal blood). If he is a II he gets blood group II. He could also take IV but as these "Universal Donors" are about only 45% of the people, we must use II's when we can. Then the proper blood is warmed in a pan of water and we are ready to start. The man is usually as white as the paper, mostly shocked, with an imperceptible pulse. He may be exsanguinated also and not so much shocked, but usually is both shocked and exsanguinated. We now inject novo-caine over the vein in the bend of the elbow, cut down and find the vein and insert a small glass Canula, then run the blood in. The change in most cases is spectacular. We give him always 500 C.C. of preserved blood and sometimes more and follow it up with saline of 5% glucose solution. The pulse can now be felt and his pale lips have some color.

Yesterday, we did three transfusions – this is about the average daily, besides the blood we leave at hospitals for them to use themselves. We collect ½ to ¾ gallon daily, mix it with Sodium Citrate (3.8%) and keep it just above freezing in the refrigerator in sterile milk and wine bottles. This blood will keep for about a week. We are working on the use of Locke's Solution to preserve the red blood cells longer and are making up Bayliss' Gum Solution. (Gum Arabic in Saline). Bayliss was (or is!) an English Physiologist who brought out this gum solution for shock during the war of 1914–18.

The International Brigade Hospital needs male and female French and German speaking nurses – not English speaking at present although these may be needed later. Brain surgeons also.

Well, this is a grand country and great people. The wounded are wonderful.

After I had given a transfusion to a French soldier who had lost his arm, he raised the other to me as I left the room in the Casualty Clearing Station, and with his raised clenched fist exclaimed "Viva la Revolution." The next boy to him was a Spaniard – a medical student, shot through the liver and stomach. When I had given him a transfusion and asked him how he felt – he said "It is nothing" – Nada! He recovered. So did the Frenchman.

Transfusion work should be given in Casualty Clearing Stations when they come out of the operating room of the 1st hospital behind the lines and before they are sent back to rear hospitals. But as Madrid is the front line, our work is mostly here although we go out 25 kilometers to other parts of the line.

I am sending you the engine plate of a German fighting plane – a Heinkel.

I sent you last month 25 posters and will send more. These posters are wonderful artistic efforts. The whole city is covered with them. They stress as you see – Anti-fascism not Anarchism, Socialism or Communism. More and more every day all parties are becoming united under the realization of this war against international fascist aggression.

I am enclosing some radio speeches. Use them when you think fit. Either singly or I would suggest together in the press or journals.

Well I will close now. We all feel enormously encouraged by your grand support. You may rest assured and give our assurance to the workers of Canada that their efforts and money are saving many Spanish, French, German and English lives. We will win – the Fascists are already defeated. Madrid will be the tomb of Fascism.

Salud, Companyeros!

Norman Bethune

P.S. I nearly forgot to mention the reason you received so little news of me in December was I gave letters to the Foreign Propaganda Chief who was arrested a week ago as a suspected spy. None were sent out! Except one I gave to an English woman going out to Paris. There are too many Fascist spies here.

N.B.
Madrid is the centre of gravity of the world and I wouldn't be anywhere else.
Please send us – Periodicals and papers.
We have seen no papers nor journals since arrival.
Was Roosevelt elected?
Please send – Montreal Gazette, Montreal Star – Toronto Star, New Masses, New Frontier, etc.
N. B. We really know nothing of the outside world.

Research file for documentary film *Bethune* (1964)
National Film Board Library, Montreal

# 5 ◆ THE *SERVICIO CANADIENSE* EXPANDS

During the first days of its operation, Bethune began to envisage a more important role for his blood transfusion service, and on a far larger stage. In the relative calm that followed the end of the campaign of early January, the location of Franco's next strike was the subject of much speculation. The area that Bethune sensed might become a battle front was the southeast coast, where Republican forces had a tenuous hold on the city of Málaga. He wondered how health officials would cope with the need for blood if the Nationalists were to launch an assault in the south. He considered that the blood transfusion service was now battle-tested. Could he not take the same type of organization and system to other areas of Republican Spain? Now, only three weeks after he had moved into his quarters at 36 Príncipe de Vergara, he decided to propose to the Socorro Rojo Internacional (SRI) a plan to extend the area served by the unit so that it could supply all Republican forces with blood.

Although they agreed in principle with Bethune's aim, SRI officials in Madrid told him that a unified Republican army under central command was quickly taking shape, and that all military health matters would soon become the responsibility of a reconstituted department, the Sanidad Militar. They made it clear to Bethune that he would have to present his proposal to officials in that department. Bethune complied. On January

Sise (middle), Bethune, and Sorensen (right) in front of the Instituto canadiense. On the Ford is the pennant of the SRI. (Photographer unknown. Roderick Stewart collection)

11, he and Sorensen set out in the Ford for Valencia. There, at the head-quarters of the Sanidad Militar, Bethune outlined his scheme to its military chief, Colonel Cerrada. Like the SRI officials, Cerrada agreed that the concept had merit, but drew Bethune's attention to two problems. The first was financial. Where would the money come from? Bethune's response was rapid. He was certain that the same source that was funding the Instituto, the Committee to Aid Spanish Democracy (CASD), would be willing to embrace this new challenge and provide financial support for it. The second was the Barcelona Blood Transfusion Service of Dr. Durán i Jordà.

It seems more than likely that Bethune had learned of Durán i Jordà sometime after taking possession of the apartment on Príncipe de Vergara in December. Realizing that Cerrada would not enter into an agreement without Durán i Jordà's participation, Bethune agreed to meet the Spanish doctor. Driving to Barcelona, he and Sorensen made their way to Hospital Number 18 in Montjuich. Durán i Jordà showed Bethune his facilities, and the two men discussed their respective techniques for collecting and storing blood. Durán i Jordà listened to Bethune's plan for a uniform service throughout the Republican sector. He found the plan generally sound and was prepared to accept it with certain modifications.

One of Durán i Jordà's trucks at his Barcelona hospital. (Photographer unknown. Roderick Stewart collection)

The major change was to make Barcelona, rather than Madrid, the collection and distribution centre. It was also obvious to Bethune that Durán i Jordà's facilities and equipment were more complex than those in the Instituto and that the method he had developed for collecting and storing blood in packaged, pressurized ampoules was superior to his own. Regarding his acceptance of Durán i Jordà's conditions as the basis for a tentative agreement, Bethune left him with a sum of 3,000 pesetas to be used to purchase equipment.

After examining the railway car and two large trucks that Durán i Jordà had equipped with refrigerators, Bethune decided to follow suit with a refrigerated truck. He was able to buy refrigerators in Barcelona, but failed to find a truck that met his requirements. On Saturday, January 16, he took an Air France flight with Sorensen to Marseille to look for a truck there. Before leaving, he sent a telegram to Hazen Sise in Madrid instructing him to leave on Sunday for Barcelona. Sise found the following letter waiting for him in the Hotel Continental:

Dear Hazen –

After a perfectly hectic 3 (or is it 4) days, the following points are clear –

1. Impossible to purchase any kind of car in Barcelona

2. The blood ampules are OK and since it's patented and [the] ... process of putting up the blood [is complicated], it can not be reproduced in Madrid, ergo – we must use Barcelona as a collecting centre for this kind of blood.

3. The manufacture will cost about 3000 pesetas a month. I have guaranteed this payment.

4. We propose to start a "shuttle" service from Barcelona to Valencia, Madrid, and Cordoba with distributing centres at these other points. Here (at the D.S.) must be installed refrigerators, distribution, staff, etc. That's a problem of the S.R.I. (and us, of course).

5. I have sent a cable to Spence asking them to send out Paterson of Montreal (an Englishman who runs a ski shop in Montreal and who wanted to come out with me at first – he is a first class chap and an excellent motor driver – has his own M.G.). The alternative I proposed was Norman McLeod of Toronto, a splendid fellow – engineer, 30. This man (either fellow) should be, with you, a two-man team on the delivery truck from Barcelona to the Front – a week's trip.

6. Henning and I will stay in Madrid and keep going on our original system plus this new idea.

7. We are leaving for Marseilles this afternoon to buy a truck (1 ton) and drive it to Barcelona. Here it will be fitted with the following to transform it into a refrigerator car –

  1. 2 electro box refrigerators running on 125 volts each (D.C.)

  2. 20 batteries

  3. dynamo and gas engine to charge batteries. All these are here and ordered and ready to be installed on our return. Your contacts here

    1. Dr. F. Duran, Hospital #18 Tel. 25901. He is the originator of the sterile ampule and has a refrigerator car for the Aragon Front. I have left him 3000 pesetas.

    2. Perez [at] General Motors factory who is going over the Ford engine, repainting car etc., changing oil, etc. etc. Speaks perfect English. G.M. on Calle de Mallorca – street car 49 (2 blocks from Sagrada Familia). He has keys.

Sise, Worsley, and Bethune, February 1937. *El crimen de la carretera Málaga–Almería.*
(Photographer unknown. National Library of Spain)

We hope to be back in 1 week. Address: American Express, Marseilles.
Salud
Beth

Library and Archives Canada
Hazen Sise fonds MG30-D388, volume 16, file 2

While Bethune and Sorensen were in Marseille buying a 2½-ton Renault truck, Sise was in Barcelona, where he met Thomas Worsley, a young Englishman who had recently arrived in Spain. A freelance writer and former teacher, Worsley was eager to make some kind of contribution to the Republican cause. Learning from Sise that Bethune needed a driver for the Renault, Worsley showed interest, and when Bethune and Sorensen returned from France in the Renault on Friday, January 22, Sise introduced them to Worsley. On the following day, Worsley accepted Bethune's invitation to join the unit.

When Sorensen had to be admitted to hospital in Barcelona with a case of bronchitis, Bethune drove the Ford to Valencia, where he met Colonel Cerrada on Monday. Cerrada listened to Bethune's description of his meeting with Durán i Jordà and of their tentative agreement to work together. When he responded that, although his superiors were in favour of a unified blood service, they now believed their budget could not support it, Bethune countered that he was certain the necessary amount could be raised in Canada. After they had discussed the costs of the various aspects of his proposal, Bethune made an offer. In addition to covering the salaries of the three Canadians, the CASD would pay for all equipment for the maintenance of the Madrid operation and, in addition, would make a substantial contribution toward the cost of a proposed distribution centre in Valencia. In return, he expected the Sanidad Militar to pay the salaries of the Spanish personnel. Cerrada agreed to draw up a contract to clearly delineate the mutual responsibilities of the CASD and the Sanidad Militar. As he cautioned Bethune, this contract could not go into effect until he obtained approval from the war ministry. Certain that government authorization was merely a matter of form, Bethune left Valencia fully convinced that his proposed unified blood transfusion system would soon be in operation. He drove to Madrid in high spirits, arriving on Wednesday, January 27, and immediately sent the following cable to the CASD:

Just returned [to] Madrid after being away two weeks organizing new service. Glad to get back. Bought 2½ ton Renault truck for three thousand dollars in Marseilles. Sise in Barcelona equipping with refrigerator dynamos batteries, etc. Our new plan enthusiastically accepted by Valencia government. Will cover all fronts. The scheme is to transport sealed ampoules by blood refrigeration train from collecting centre at Barcelona to main distributing points [in] Valencia. From thence to ten selected front line points three thousand kilometres apart. This is first time in history such long distance covered. Also maintaining original organization working perfectly on Madrid front. Need another driver. Cars named Tim and Ben. I received the three thousand originally sent to Valencia and from there transferred to Paris. I received the two thousand dollars sent direct to Paris and also the additional one thousand sent to Paris a day later making amount received to that date six thousand dollars. I also received the one thousand dollars. You may send unlimited quantities condensed milk and coffee. Canned goods of nearly any kind would be acceptable. Advise against the sending of old clothes. If clothes or other goods are sent they should be addressed Socorro Rojo Valencia. I am favorable to the proposition of making new clothes and sending. The amount I need weekly to effectively maintain the blood transfusion project would be about two hundred dollars. What funds not needed for the blood transfusion project I could use to advantage in other ways. No Spanish workers delegation available. Would welcome Canadians. Have not touched Paris December credits. Keep in reserve there* (see note). Reason silence either nothing new report or censor forbids. For Lenin's sake be reasonable. Working eighteen hours day. Can't be war correspondent and doctor too. Sent you three letters from France. Impossible register address. Salud

*These amount to fifteen hundred dollars to Dec. 31. In January fifteen hundred dollars more was sent besides one thousand sent to Marseilles.

Tamiment Library, New York University
Fredericka Martin Papers, ALBA 001

Interior of the Renault ambulance. (Hazen Sise. Library and Archives Canada PA-117448)

Despite the progress Bethune outlined in his cable to the CASD, various problems had developed in his two-and-a-half week absence from the Instituto that required his attention. As a result, he had to remain in Madrid for four days before being able to return to Valencia, where he hoped to work out the final details of his plan for the blood transfusion service. The most important problem in Madrid was the lack of money for the Instituto personnel. While he was in Barcelona and Marseille, he had not made adequate provision for the staff's salaries. Apologizing for the oversight, he assured them that he was on the verge of instituting a new plan of organization that would provide a regulated income for them. Although not entirely convinced, the Spaniards had no option but to accept his promise.

Bethune set out again for Valencia on January 31. At a meeting on the following day, Cerrada informed him he had still not received government approval for the agreement they had reached the previous week. Then he turned to another matter. A fundamental change in the structure of military health services was going to take place in the very near future, the aim of which was to place all health facilities and personnel in the Republican sector under the exclusive control of the Sanidad Militar. That would include, of course, the Madrid blood unit, but Cerrada quickly pointed out that the only change would be the title: it would now be named Instituto hispano-canadiense. Bethune would remain in charge of operating the unit, with the honorary rank of *comandante* (major), and both Sorensen and Sise would be recognized as captains. Cerrada ended the meeting by promising to check again with his government superiors on the agreement. He told Bethune to come back on February 6, when he expected to have confirmation.

Despite Cerrada's words of assurance, Bethune immediately recognized that the change would be fundamental. His transfusion service had been autonomous for two months, and he had hoped that this autonomy would extend to his proposed unified service. To his chagrin, he realized that from now on he would become responsible to the Sanidad Militar. It is hard to explain how he had ignored the warnings of officials of the SRI, who had clearly indicated that the stripping of authority of all militia units as part of the process of creating a unified Republican army had been taking place since December. Still, he left the meeting with Cerrada convinced that it would be only a matter of time before his plan could go into operation. Fully aware that Cerrada would not respond to his proposal for four more days, he sent the following cable to the CASD. It was published a week later in Canada:

We have succeeded in unifying all remaining Spanish transfusion units under us. We are serving 100 hospitals and casualty clearing stations in the front lines of Madrid and 100 kilometres from the front of the sector Del Centro.

The new name of the Canadian Medical Unit is Instituto Hispano-Canadiense de Transfusion de Sangre. I have been appointed director-in-chief as a grateful tribute to Canadian workers and have been given the military rank of commandante.

Sise and Sorensen have been appointed captains. We now have a staff of twenty-five, composed of haematologist, bacteriologist, five Spanish doctors, three assistants, six nurses, four technicians, chauffeurs and servants.

Sorensen is an invaluable liaison officer. Sise is operating the refrigeration truck on the southern fronts. Collected and gave ten gallons of blood during January. Expect to increase this to twenty-five gallons during this month.

This is the first unified blood transfusion service in army and medical history. Plans are well under way to supply the entire Spanish anti-fascist army preserved blood. Your institute is now operating on a 1,000 kilometre front.

I must leave for Paris immediately to buy fifty additional transfusion apparatuses. The Madrid Defence Junta has given us two new cars. We now have five cars operating here day and night in this sector.

I have contracted with an English professional photographer to make a movie film of the work of the Institute for the Canadian public.

Madrid is the centre of gravity of the world. All are well and happy.

No pasaran (They shall not pass)!

Salud Camaradas y Compañeros

*Daily Clarion* [Toronto], 9 February 1937

Bethune then sent a telegram to the other members of the unit in Barcelona telling them to come to Valencia and to bring with them several ampoules of blood from Durán i Jordà's hospital. When Sise and Worsley arrived in Valencia on Friday, February 5 in the Renault, leaving behind the still-ailing Sorensen, Bethune told them he hoped to win final approval for his plan from Cerrada at a meeting set for the following morning. After the meeting they would leave Valencia and drive south along the coastal road to the city of Málaga, which was at the southern limit of Republican control and the most distant point from Barcelona where blood would be supplied. In that way he could determine the quality of the roads, inspect hospitals along the route, explain the coming of the new transfusion service, and deliver any of the bottles of blood, should they be needed. This would also be an apt way to test the refitted Renault on a route that it would follow in the future.

At noon on Saturday, Bethune emerged from a brief meeting with Cerrada to tell Sise and Worsley that Cerrada claimed his superiors still had not reached a decision. Cerrada's response, Bethune sensed, reflected the Sanidad Militar's policy of taking control of all health facilities, and, although Cerrada had not admitted it, Bethune felt certain the Spaniards had firmly decided that now was not the time to give a foreigner control over the proposed expansion of the blood transfusion service. It is also certain that Durán i Jordà would not have accepted a role inferior to Bethune's, given that the latter's qualifications in hematology were clearly unequal to his. One other factor may have been Cerrada's personal assessment of Bethune. Bethune had devised his plan to serve his only concern – to save lives – and had discussed it in detail during two lengthy conferences with Cerrada. He believed that he had answered all possible objections. Unable to understand that others might not see things his way, he may have revealed his impatience of bureaucratic snags in a manner that offended Cerrada.

# 6 ◆ THE MÁLAGA–ALMERÍA ROAD

Disappointed though he was that the Sanidad Militar had not yet approved his plan, Bethune still wanted to make the trip to Málaga. He knew the background of the conflict in the south. Málaga, a city of 100,000, was in the centre of a thirty-kilometre-wide sliver of Republican territory lying between the Mediterranean and the Sierra Nevada and ending a few kilometres north of Gibraltar. To the west, and on the north side of the mountains, was Nationalist territory. Over the past few months, the population of the city had grown significantly as a result of the arrival of thousands of refugees fleeing the advance of Nationalist troops in neighbouring provinces. Málaga had become a closed alley; the only land route out was a narrow road that wound along the rugged seacoast to the port of Almería, nearly 200 kilometres to the east.

The Nationalist forces were commanded by General Queipo de Llano, known for his nightly radio talks. His barbaric threats delighted the Nationalists and sharpened the edge of fear among Republicans. In one broadcast he ranted: "If any fag, any pervert, spreads alarming lies, do not hesitate to kill him like a dog … I remind all of them that for every decent person who dies, I will shoot, at least, ten of them, and there are towns where we have gone higher than that number … I authorize you to kill, like a dog, anyone who dares to threaten you; and if you do so, you will be freed from any blame."

Bethune driving the Ford. (Photographer unknown. Roderick Stewart collection)

From the outset of the uprising, the Nationalists were intent on creating a state of fear and intimidation among people in areas that remained loyal to the Republic. On July 19, the second day of the revolt, the Nationalist general Emilio Mola said: "It is necessary to create an atmosphere of terror ... Anyone who is openly or secretly a defender of the Popular Front (Republican supporters) must be shot." Rape, and the threat of rape, were used with impunity as a weapon of war. Queipo de Llano condoned this practice: "Our brave Legionnaires and Regulars have demonstrated to the cowardly reds [Republicans] what it means to truly be a man. And the same for their women. This is fully justified because these communists and anarchists preach free love. Now, at least they will know what true men are and not homosexual militiamen."

Fortunately for the people of the region, Franco's fixation on Madrid had initially left the area around Málaga relatively untouched. However, in mid-January an offensive led by Nationalist units and assisted by a detachment of nearly 10,000 Italian Blackshirts had broken through at several points along the periphery of the Republican territory. During the next ten days, these forces had moved toward Málaga. What Bethune did not know was that, despite the arrival of refugees driven into the city by

"They were of all ages, but their faces were drawn with the same features of suffering" (Norman Bethune). (Norman Bethune. Library and Archives Canada PA-117543)

the advance of the enemy, Republican military authorities seemed indifferent to the danger of their position until February 5. On that date, Nationalist warships appeared to the west of Málaga and began to shell Republican forces along the coastline.

Poorly equipped and badly organized militia units immediately began to flee toward the city, followed only a few kilometres behind by Nationalist soldiers. On Saturday, while awareness of the imminent arrival of the enemy spread quickly through the city, the military authorities under the command of Colonel José Villalba dithered about what to do. At hastily convened meetings, Communist and Anarchist militia leaders accused the authorities of treachery. Only the governor of the province actually did something: silently, without informing anyone, he abandoned Málaga in the middle of the afternoon.

At about 9:00 o'clock on Sunday evening Bethune and his companions left Valencia. He was in the Ford, and Sise and Worsley were in the Renault. Running into a raging sandstorm about 200 kilometres out of Valencia, they stopped at Alicante at 2:00 a.m. and found a room in a small hotel.

The commandant of a hospital that Bethune visited in the morning told him of an unconfirmed report that Málaga had fallen. Bethune immediately alerted his companions, and together they left Alicante at 10:30 a.m. for Murcia. There, in the late afternoon, after they had checked into a hotel, Bethune began to visit local hospitals to inspect them and discuss his blood transfusion scheme with the military medical authorities. His inspections continued the following day.

On the morning of Wednesday, February 10, Bethune and his companions left at dawn in the Renault on the next leg of their journey to the seaport town of Almería, more than 200 kilometres away. Deciding that it was not necessary to continue with two vehicles, Bethune had made arrangements to leave the Ford in Murcia until their return from the south. In Almería he went directly to the local hospital, where SRI officials assured him that the fall of Málaga was not a rumour.

Málaga had, in fact, fallen on Monday. The early Sunday morning silence had been broken by the sound of artillery and machine-gun bursts, and on the near horizon appeared three warships, which began to shell the city. Soon airplanes arrived, dropping not bombs but leaflets containing a brief message signed by General Queipo de Llano: "Malagueñans, this message is directed primarily to the militiamen who have been misled. The die is cast and you have lost. In a few hours a circle of steel will crush you." On the highway descending from the mountains that enclosed Málaga, a long line of army trucks came into view.

Just past five o'clock, with public fear growing rapidly, the chief of staff of the Republican Army of the South and his senior officers fled from the city without notice. Soon rumours spread that signs had been posted on the doors of the now-closed government offices, which said, "Every man for himself!" Cries of "the Moors are coming, the Moors are coming" echoed throughout the city as people panicked at the news that General Franco's feared North African troops were upon them. By nightfall the streets were jammed with people in a flood that gathered at the port and twisted toward the east, toward the highway to Almería, the only possible way out. Seized by panic and caught up in the collective hysteria, 100,000 people began the flight amid darkness and chaos. On Monday morning, Italian and Nationalist troops entered Málaga unopposed.

Meanwhile, confirmed reports of sea and air attacks on refugees fleeing Málaga also indicated that Italian troops were moving rapidly along the coastal highway behind the refugees toward the town of Motril. From early Monday morning until late on Wednesday night, a combination of Nationalist planes and warships pursued the refugees, periodically attacking them. Fighter planes banked low to strafe the solid masses of fugitives, while from the sea a cruiser and a destroyer fired salvos at them. Whenever the sound of an airplane was heard, everyone would try to run off the road, hoping for safety behind large rocks, or to escape the range of tracer fire. Some were lucky. Others were riddled with bullets or blown to pieces by shelling from the warships. With the aid of powerful searchlights, the two ships were able to keep the refugees under attack at night. For nearly three days the Nationalist slaughter continued without Republican opposition.

"Thousands of children. The mothers carried them across their shoulders, or led them by the hand. A man went by with his two little ones on his back, children one and two years old" (Norman Bethune). (Hazen Sise. National Film Board of Canada)

Learning of the fall of Málaga, Bethune acted quickly. Doctors would be needed, he told his companions. At 3:30 p.m, with Bethune at the wheel of the Renault, they left Almería, heading west along the coastal road. After only a few kilometres they began to see small groups of people, some of them entire families, moving slowly along the roadside, their possessions slung over the back of a weary mule. At first, the groups were separated by distances of nearly 100 metres, but soon the gap narrowed until there was an unbroken line that gradually widened as people spilled out onto the highway, forcing Bethune to drive closer to the side of the road. These were the first refugees on foot, now nearing the end of their 200-kilometre trek from Málaga.

About fifteen kilometres out of Almería the road veered inland and rose steeply to the crest of a hill, from which it led down to a vast plain. Bethune stopped the Renault; the three men got out to have a look. Stretching before them as far as they could see in the late afternoon sunlight, a distance of nearly twenty kilometres, was a long black line snaking through the centre of the plain. It was the road, covered from side to side with fugitives from Málaga. They resumed their journey; Bethune now had to keep his hand on the horn as they slowly made their way through the masses of people. As their speed declined they noticed more details. The fugitives were covered with dust. Many were shoeless – some with rags tied around their feet, others with no protection at all against the stony white road. Mothers held babies in their arms, and many a father plodded along with a child draped across his shoulders. Most of the refugees had not eaten since they had left Málaga.

Soon Bethune saw a troop of cavalry ahead, and then larger and larger groups of militiamen, their uniforms dirty and torn, their eyes fixed downward as they silently shuffled along. When the last of the soldiers, which they estimated at more than three thousand, had passed them, they slowed to a halt in the hope of questioning the civilians. No one would stop. A few paused long enough to point back along the road, utter the word "Fascists," and move on. Each was gripped by the fear of being overtaken by the pursuing enemy forces. All had but one aim: to reach what they believed was the haven of Almería.

Bethune and the others stood in the road beside the Renault debating what to do while the human stream flowed around them. Sise lamented

Mother and child on the Málaga–Almería road. (Hazen Sise. National Film Board of Canada)

that they had no weapons to defend themselves, and Worsley pointed out that if they did meet an advance unit of the Italian Blackshirts, the necessity to turn the large Renault around on a highway covered with refugees would make them easy targets. But Bethune pointed to the inscription on the side of the Renault: *Servicio canadiense de transfusión de sangre al frente.* "See that, boys?" he said. "Service at the front. To the front we go." Then he clambered into the Renault and started the engine. Without another word, Sise and Worsley got in and they started off again.

At first, the growing awareness of the extent of the tragedy that they were witnessing numbed them into silence, but gradually they began to draw one another's attention to disturbing sights – people staggering under heavy burdens, forced to the side of the moving throng; elderly men and women who had given up and collapsed at the edge of the road. All of this affected Bethune, but it was the plight of the children that moved him the most. Through much of the distance he had tried to keep a count of the children under ten years of age and the number of those who were shoeless, their bare feet swollen or wrapped in bloodied rags. They numbered in the thousands.

Near nightfall, Bethune and his companions were nearly twenty kilometres short of Motril. Bethune suddenly stopped the Renault. He told the others that he had decided to turn the vehicle around, fill it with children, and drive them back to Almería.

As long as they remained inside the Renault, they had been isolated, spectators of a procession that was passing outside their bubble of security. But as soon as they opened the doors, left their vehicle, and mixed with the throng, they found themselves enveloped in the atmosphere of the highway, overflowing with panic and misery.

The moment Bethune opened the back doors of the Renault, a throng of refugees gathered around him. Aware that a miraculous opportunity was presenting itself, the mute, suffering people came to life, shouting, crying, reaching out, begging for a place in the vehicle. Bethune tried to accept only children, but was unable to separate them from their mothers. In a matter of minutes the truck was crammed with nearly forty women and children. Bethune slammed the doors shut. Turning to Sise, he told him to drive the refugees to Almería as fast as he could and then return for him and Worsley. Meanwhile, they would join the crowd moving toward Almería.

For about an hour Bethune and Worsley tramped along the road with the multitude. When Bethune began to tire they tried to sleep under a group of palm trees; sleep was impossible, and they soon resumed the march. Around midnight, Bethune noticed a stable not far from the road. Inside they found enough straw for a makeshift bed, and Bethune fell asleep immediately. Worsley, unable to tolerate the stench of the dung that covered the floor, joined a group gathered outside around a fire. Several hours later he and Bethune returned to the road. Just before dawn, they saw the headlights of the approaching Renault. From the point where Sise had left them on Wednesday night, Bethune and Worsley had walked seventeen kilometres.

Bethune and Worsley flagged Sise down. He told them that no provision had been made for food or shelter for the refugees flooding into Almería. The city was in chaos. He had taken the women and children to the Socorro Rojo hospital, filled the gas tank, and made a slow return

"We stopped the truck, unloaded the equipment and then opened the back doors.
We could see the excitement on the faces of the refugees" (Norman Bethune).
(Hazen Sise. National Film Board of Canada)

Worsley driving, with Sise on his right. The Renault was loaded with refugees, some clinging to the fenders. (Norman Bethune. Library and Archives Canada PA-117452)

journey along the still-clogged highway. Noticing that Sise, who had not slept, was obviously exhausted, Bethune decided that Sise should go with Worsley while he took a second load of refugees to Almería. After dropping the women and children off at the hospital, Worsley would leave Sise at the hotel to get some sleep while he drove back to pick up Bethune on the highway.

When Sise and Worsley reached Almería, the Civil Governor, learning that Bethune's team had witnessed what was happening on the highway, asked them to describe the situation. Their reply stunned him. They then warned him to get ready to receive some 100,000 people and implored him to send trucks to deliver food and blankets and to collect refugees on the road between Almería and Motril. The Governor's response shocked them in turn: "How am I going to send nothing?" he demanded. "I don't have any food. Before we were scraping by with very little, but now there

74

is nothing! As for trucks, first I have to bring back the troops. Soldiers are my priority."

Meanwhile, now just one figure more among the many thousands, Bethune trudged along the coastal road. At a short distance east of the village of Castell de Ferro, he heard the sound of airplanes. Turning, he gazed up into the clear afternoon sky to see three fighter planes attacking two small bombers. He recognized the attackers as Italian Fiats. Suddenly, smoke trailed from the engine of one of the bombers. As the plane headed for the water, Bethune ran down the rocky hillside to the beach and joined a small crowd gathered on the shore. Militiamen had already waded into the shallow water to help the crew of the downed aircraft, which Bethune later learned was a Potez – one of the last two of the squadron formed in 1936 by André Malraux. Two crew members were unharmed, but five were seriously injured and were laid on the sand. Despite his lack of Spanish, Bethune managed to identify himself as a doctor. He rapidly examined the wounded, two of whom were bleeding badly. Wading out to the plane, he ripped out some wires to use as tourniquets. Then he led the militiamen who were carrying the wounded up the hill to the highway, where he somehow commandeered a truck. With the wounded inside and Bethune standing on the running board, the vehicle headed for Almería, more than eighty kilometres away.

It was not long before Bethune saw the Renault approaching, driven by Worsley. When Worsley pulled up, Bethune quickly explained what had happened and told him to return to the spot near the stable where they had spent part of Wednesday night, fill the truck with refugees, and return to Almería. Worsley followed Bethune's instructions, but on his return the Renault broke down, stranding him and his passengers on the road until early Friday morning, when a truck towed them into Almería.

Bethune continued on to Almería with the wounded. However, he was without medical instruments and the distance was too great. Before they reached Almería in the early evening, the co-pilot succumbed to his wounds, and in the Socorro Rojo hospital in Almería, surgeons were forced to amputate one arm of another crew member. In the same hospital Bethune subsequently performed transfusions on other members of the crew, using blood brought from Barcelona. Unfortunately, the men died, whether from their wounds or, as Sise suspected, from the blood

Refugees in Almería. Hazen Sise. (Library and Archives Canada PA-117425)

itself, which may have been spoiled by repeated shaking as the Renault drove over the rugged coastal road.

Reunited in Almería, Bethune, Sise, and Worsley encountered Adrian Phillips, a representative of the International Red Cross. When Bethune discovered that Phillips had no idea of the calamity that had unfolded over the past five days, and showed no interest in taking steps to find food and medical supplies for the refugees, he insisted that Phillips drive along the Málaga road to see the scope of the disaster for himself. Phillips reluctantly agreed to do so, and also to take Sise in his car. At some point along the road, he would drop off Sise to allow him to spend several hours taking photographs, as Sise wished to record the tragedy occurring on the Málaga road. When the repairs to the Renault were completed, Bethune and Worsley would drive out and pick Sise up.

By 7:00 p.m. the Renault was still being repaired. As Bethune and Worsley watched the mechanic, the lights suddenly went out and a siren

Bethune helping refugees into the Renault near La Rábita. (Hazen Sise. Library and Archives Canada PA-124407)

sounded. Seconds later the ground began to shake as a series of thunderous explosions rent the air. Grabbing Worsley, Bethune pulled him down to the floor and shouted at him to cover his head as a shower of stone, metal, and glass rained down on them. The deafening bombardment continued for several minutes, and then stopped. After a few seconds of silence, Bethune and Worsley began to hear screams. Raising their heads, they saw a reddish-orange glow suffusing everything. Making their way to the door, they stepped into the street to see several buildings only a block away engulfed in flames. Bethune immediately yanked Worsley's arm and started running toward the burning buildings. Followed by Worsley, pushing his way through the crowds of terrified, stunned people, Bethune kept yelling *"Médico! Médico!"* Ahead of them a bomb had destroyed a house. Screaming people covered with blood were trapped beneath jagged pieces of masonry, shattered timber, and a tangle of electrical wires. For the next six hours Bethune worked with others, doing what he could to assist the helpless victims. The savage incendiary attack had been carried out by a squad of the German Condor Legion, the same force that two months later would bombard the town of Guérnica. Although their bombs did slight damage to the Republican cruiser *Jaime I* in the harbour, their principal target was the mass of helpless refugees jammed into the city.

At 2:00 a.m., after doing what he could for the victims of the bombing, Bethune returned to the hotel to sleep. Later that morning, with the Renault repaired, he drove west with Worsley on the Málaga road. By early afternoon, they picked up Sise some fifty kilometres west of Almería and continued along the road to Motril, meeting fewer and fewer refugees until, rounding a bend, they were surprised to find that the road ahead was clear for as far as they could see. They drove on a few more kilometres before recognizing that they had passed the last refugee from Málaga. At this point, both Worsley and Sise expected Bethune to turn around, but he resolutely insisted that they complete what they had set out to do on Wednesday. He was determined to reach Motril, where, he argued, there would likely be refugees in need of medical treatment. They continued to a point about fifteen kilometres from Motril where a military barrier was stretched across the road. Only when an officer turned them back, insisting that medical personnel in Motril were attending to those in need, did Bethune tell Worsley to turn the Renault around. Catching up with the last refugees, they stopped, filled the vehicle with women and children, and made their way back to Almería, where they pulled up in front of the hospital just before midnight. This was their last load of refugees.

That night Bethune was unable to sleep. Since leaving Almería on Wednesday afternoon, he had seen much that had revolted him. But the enormity of this attack on innocent civilians, and particularly children, evoked sheer rage in him. He had seen parts of what, many years later, would be recognized as the most heinous atrocity of the war, and he burned to express his revulsion at the Fascists' savage treatment of helpless human beings. During the next few hours he wrote an impassioned account of the three days that he and his companions had spent in their efforts to assist the refugees from Málaga. Entitled *The Crime on the Road: Málaga–Almería*, it was later published as a pamphlet and used as a powerful instrument of persuasion.

In Almería, discussing the situation of the refugees. (Hazen Sise. Roderick Stewart collection)

The evacuation en masse of the civilian population of Malaga started on Sunday Feb. 7. Twentyfive thousand German, Italian and Moorish troops entered the town on Monday morning the eighth. Tanks, submarines, warships, airplanes combined to smash the defenses of the city held by a small heroic band of Spanish troops without tanks, airplanes or support. The so-called Nationalists entered, as they have entered every captured village and city in Spain, what was practically a deserted town.

Now imagine one hundred and fifty thousand men, women and children setting out for safety to the town situated over a hundred miles away. There is only one road they can take. There is no other way of escape. This road, bordered on one side by the high Sierra Nevada mountains and on the other by the sea, is cut into the side of the cliffs and climbs up and down from sea-level to over 500 feet. The city they must reach is Almeria, and it is over two hundred kilometers away. A strong, healthy young man can walk on foot forty or fifty kilometers a day. The journey these women, children and old

Men and women trudging along. (Hazen Sise. Library and Archives Canada PA-117544)

people must face will take five days and five nights at least. There will be no food to be found in the villages, no trains, no buses to transport them. They must walk and as they walked, staggered and stumbled with cut, bruised feet along that flint, white road the fascists bombed them from the air and fired at them from their ships at sea.

Now, what I want to tell you is what I saw myself of this forced march – the largest, most terrible evacuation of a city in modern times. We had arrived in Almeria at five o'clock on Wednesday the tenth with a refrigeration truckload of preserved blood from Barcelona. Our intention was to proceed to Malaga to give blood transfusions to wounded. In Almeria we heard for the first time that the town had fallen and were warned to go no farther as no one knew where the frontline now was but everyone was sure that the town of Motril had also fallen. We thought it important to proceed and discover how the evacuation of the wounded was proceeding. We set out at six o'clock in the evening along the Malaga road and a few miles on we met the head of the piteous procession. Here were the strong with all their goods on

Worsley helping refugees into the Renault. (Hazen Sise. National Film Board of Canada)

donkeys, mules and horses. We passed them, and the farther we went the more pitiful the sights became. Thousands of children, we counted five thousand under ten years of age, and at least one thousand of them barefoot and many of them clad only in a single garment. They were slung over their mother's shoulders or clung to her hands. Here a father staggered along with two children of one and two years of age on his back in addition to carrying pots and pans or some treasured possession. The incessant stream of people became so dense we could barely force the car through them. At eighty eight kilometers from Almeria they beseeched us to go no farther, that the fascists were just behind. By this time we had passed so many distressed women and children that we thought it best to turn back and start transporting the worst cases to safety.

It was difficult to choose which to take. Our car was besieged by a mob of frantic mothers and fathers who with tired outstretched arms held up to us their children, their eyes and faces swollen and congested by four days of sun and dust.

"My thoughts were interrupted by a strange procession. I looked out the window with curiosity. Were they peasants? Yes, walking with their donkeys" (Norman Bethune). Hazen Sise. (Library and Archives Canada PA-117543)

"Take this one." "See this child." "This one is wounded." Children with bloodstained rags wrapped around their arms and legs, children without shoes, their feet swollen to twice their size crying helplessly from pain, hunger and fatigue. Two hundred kilometers of misery. Imagine four days and four nights, hiding by day in the hills as the fascist barbarians pursued them by plane, walking by night packed in a solid stream men, women, children, mules, donkeys, goats, crying out the names of their separated relatives, lost in the mob. How could we chose between taking a child dying of dysentery or a mother silently watching us with great sunken eyes carrying against her open breast her child born on the road two days ago. She had stopped walking for ten hours only. Here was a woman of sixty unable to stagger another step, her gigantic swollen legs with their open varicose ulcers bleeding into her cut linen sandals. Many old people simply gave up the struggle, lay down by the side of the road and waited for death.

We first decided to take only children and mothers. Then the separation between father and child, husband and wife became too cruel to bear. We finished by transporting families with the largest number of young children and the solitary children of which there were hundreds without parents. We carried thirty to forty people a trip for the next three days and nights back to Almeria to the hospital of the Socorro Rojo International where they received medical attention, food and clothing. The tireless devotion of Hazen Sise and Thomas Worsley, drivers of the truck, saved many lives. In turn they drove back and forth day and night sleeping out on the open road between shifts with no food except dry bread and oranges.

And now comes the final barbarism. Not content with bombing and shelling this procession of unarmed peasants on this long road, on the evening of the 12th when the little seaport of Almeria was completely filled with refugees, its population swollen to double its size, when forty thousand exhausted people had reached a haven of what they thought was safety, we were heavily bombed by German and Italian fascist airplanes. The siren alarm sounded thirty seconds before the first bomb fell. These planes made no effort to hit the government battleship in the harbor or bomb the barracks. They deliberately dropped ten great bombs in the very center of the town where on the main street were sleeping huddled together on the pavement so closely that a car could pass only with difficulty, the exhausted refugees. After the planes had passed I picked up in my arms three dead children from the pavement in front of the Provincial Committee for the Evacuation of Refugees where they had been standing in a great queue waiting for a cupful of preserved milk and a handful of dry bread, the only food some of them had for days. The street was a shambles of the dead and dying, lit only by the orange glare of burning buildings. In the darkness the moans of the wounded children, shrieks of agonized mothers, the curses of the men rose in a massed cry higher and higher to a pitch of intolerable intensity. One's body felt as heavy as the dead themselves, but empty and hollow, and in one's brain burned a bright flame of hate. That night were murdered fifty civilians and an additional fifty were wounded. There were two soldiers killed.

Now, what was the crime that these unarmed civilians had committed to be murdered in this bloody manner? Their only crime was that they had voted to elect a government of the people, committed to the most moderate alleviation of the crushing burden of centuries of the greed of capitalism. The question has been raised: – why did they not stay in Malaga and await the entrance of the fascists? They knew what would happen to them. They

"At that moment five fascist airplanes appeared and began to bomb the road" (Norman Bethune). (Hazen Sise. Roderick Stewart collection)

"There were many children. There were families that carried children who weren't their own" (Cristóbal Criado, refugee). (Hazen Sise. National Film Board of Canada)

knew what would happen to their men and women as had happened so many times before in other captured towns. Every male between the age of 15 and 60 who could not prove that he had not by force been made to assist the government would immediately be shot. And it is this knowledge that has concentrated two-thirds of the entire population of Spain in one half the country and that still held by the republic.

*The Crime on the Road Malaga–Almeria*
Madrid; Publicaciones Iberia, [1937]
Osler Library of the History of Medicine, McGill University
Norman Bethune Collection P156, accession 445B, folder 3

# 7  ◆  NEW PROJECTS

Returning to Murcia on February 15 with Sise and Worsley, Bethune picked up the Ford and told his companions to drive to Madrid in the Renault and inform the staff of the Instituto hispano-canadiense that he was on his way to Paris to collect money to pay their salaries. Before leaving, he drove to Valencia where, after cabling the CASD to send more money to Paris, he went to the offices of the Sanidad Militar. He outlined his experiences of the last ten days and asked Colonel Cerrada once again if a decision had been reached about his proposed blood transfusion service. The negative response he received tested Bethune's self-control, but he realized there was nothing he could do to force the Sanidad Militar to act.

Never easily discouraged and always averse to inactivity, Bethune was used to conceiving new projects and putting them into operation. At this point he decided to test a new idea. He reached Paris late Friday evening in the Ford, and the following morning contacted Peter Rhodes, a United Press International correspondent he knew. When he told Rhodes that he wanted to make a film about the Instituto and needed a photographer, Rhodes suggested a young Hungarian, Geza Kárpáthi, to whom he introduced Bethune later that day. After Kárpáthi produced some samples of his work, Bethune hired him as his photographer and gave him money

"The avalanche of refugees were all the same, all were worn out. So great was the fear that if they saw a crow in the distance they thought it was a plane and people cried out in terror" (Miguel Escalona, refugee). (Hazen Sise. Library and Archives Canada PA-117424)

to buy a camera and other equipment, to be entrusted to the Spanish embassy in Paris for shipment to Madrid.

After these arrangements were made, Bethune held a lengthy discussion with Gertrude Araquistáin, the wife of the ambassador. The disaster on the Málaga–Almería road had intensified his concern for the effects of the war on the civilian population, particularly children. For the past several days an idea to create refuges for displaced children had been forming in his mind. If the Sanidad Militar eventually took total control of the blood transfusion service, he began to think, the money raised in Canada for the Instituto could then be directed to building what he termed a "Children's City." After listening to Bethune describe his proposal, Señora Araquistáin asked him for a detailed outline of his ideas. Bethune returned to his hotel and dashed off a cable to Sise, very briefly describing his ideas and telling him to go to Barcelona to ask some architects that Sise knew there to begin drawing up plans for a refuge for children in the foothills of the Pyrenees. Then he summarized his thinking in the following memorandum, which he delivered to the Spanish embassy:

Señora Araquistain:

In view of the large number of Spanish children, many of whom are orphans, who are now refugees in the provinces of Valencia and Catalonia, a situation has arisen which would seem to demand a new method of handling the placement of these children.

At present, placement of the children is done under the following heads.
In Spain:
    1. In private families.
    2. In existing institutions
    3. In newly-created institutions
Abroad:
    4. In private families
    5. In existing institutions
    6. In newly-organized institutions.
Comments on the above
1. This would seem to be, at first glance, a most satisfactory solution of the problem but in reality it is far from such. Some of the difficulties are:
    (a) lack of adequate investigation of families as to their suitability to receive children
    (b) difficulties of control
    (c) often poor economic, educational and cultural environment make such families unsuitable though willing to receive children
2. These existing institutions (orphanages, schools and crèches) are crowded to paucity, their buildings are congested and their staffs overworked. Enlargement of these institutions is not contemplated. This method is the one which should be adopted with its centralization under the control – the state. (It is here proposed that the Spanish Government should build and erect the first institution of its kind in the world ... a complete Children's City, to house, educate and train 25,000

"Everyone was shouting and pushing. They told us that the wounded should come first and, because my aunt and her mother were injured, they put them in the truck. I remained alone and lost" (Ana Pérez, refugee). (Hazen Sise. National Film Board of Canada)

children between the ages of one and sixteen years. Details of this scheme will be outlined.

3. We are strongly opposed to this method. Separation from parents, homesickness, loss of contact with Spanish cultural life and the pernicious implantation of bourgeois ideals, all make it unsatisfactory from every point of view. It should be abandoned immediately.

4. Much the same objections as to No. 4, to which are especially added those objections which are applied to the defects of the bourgeois education system and the interference of bodies who control such institutions.

5. The only permissible foreign placement scheme, it nevertheless has

serious defects; such as the interference of voluntary bodies who would be financially interested.

6. To all foreign placement schemes the same general objection is raised – namely, the removal to foreign countries long distances away, separation from parents, loss of Spanish cultural ideas, bourgeois contamination and interference by foreign, well-meaning but often stupid advisers, and lastly – the impossibility of complete Spanish governmental control.

The problem must be faced with a long-range view to the future society and the imperative need of educating those children who will be its citizens.

Centralization is necessary both from the point of view of economy, and standardization and control. It is proposed under this concept of the children's City to unify all institutions now caring for refugee children under the control of the state. Some of the ideas which are suggested follow.

1. This city shall be planned in the fullest detail by the Barcelona group of architects who were responsible for the modern workmen's flats and apartments in that city.

2. It shall be located either in Catalonia or the province of Valencia, preferably in a sheltered valley with natural water supply and drainage and on a main rail line.

3. The types of buildings should be such as employed during the last European war for the housing of troops, or, such improved designs as have been made since then. Materials like corrugated iron, compressed wood and synthetic fabrics such as are used in American "knock-down" house could be used.

4. The city will contain its own schools, occupational and training workshops, theatres, gymnasiums and playgrounds. It should be divided into various quarters. ([The] quarters might be called the English, French, German, Italian quarters and each country would be responsible for the erection and maintenance of its own quarter.) The streets in the quarters should be named after prominent anti-fascist leaders in the countries. The names of the blocks and subsections should be made to correspond to particular towns or cities in the various countries so that these cities would have a personal interest in giving monetary support.

(An example – The town of Winnipeg, Manitoba, in Canada would have a Winnipeg block on Tim Buck Avenue in the Canadian quarter.) In this Winnipeg block individual organizations could have special projects such

"We suffered much hunger. We ate what we could: sugar cane, vegetables from the fields" (Cristóbal Criado, refugee). *El crimen de la carretera Málaga–Almería.* (Hazen Sise. National Library of Spain)

as a house, school or park named after their organizations.)

5. Medical and dental societies of the various countries could be appealed to in projects pertaining to the physical welfare of the children, rehabilitation of defectives and general health work.

6. Advice from the leading Russian civic planning and educational advisers should be welcomed. Also, where such would be found suitable, the latest development in American and English systems should be incorporated. These last would be valuable from the point of view of organization.

The outline of the scheme given above is submitted to your approval with the expectation that such a scheme is not only desirable but highly practicable. It should be given the greatest publicity in every country of the world by press, radio and visiting delegates. I feel sure that its success would be beyond our most enthusiastic expectations as such an appeal for refugee children is removed from the sphere of conflicting political ideologies and goes directly to the great heart of humanity.

[signed]
Dr. Norman Bethune
Comandante Sanidad Militar, Chief of the Hispano-Canadian Institute for the Transfusion of Blood.

Tamiment Library, New York University<br>Fredericka Martin Papers, ALBA 001

On the day after Bethune's arrival in Paris, Allen May, a young Canadian journalist, arrived at his hotel room. May had been sent by the CASD to join the unit as an office manager, a position that the CASD hoped would allow him to report on expenditures, details of which they believed Bethune had never adequately provided. After collecting the funds cabled from Toronto and making various purchases for himself and the Instituto, Bethune left Paris with May in the Ford.

On February 26 they arrived at the Hotel Continental in Barcelona. There, they met Sise and Worsley, who had followed Bethune's instructions to go there from Madrid. In Bethune's room, while they were drinking whisky Bethune had brought from Paris, Sise admitted he had not contacted any architects in Barcelona, as Bethune had asked. When Sise went on to explain that the brevity of the telegram made it difficult to understand precisely what was wanted, Bethune enthusiastically launched into a lengthy description of his plan, which he illustrated with a series of drawings as he talked.

After he had finished, Sise mentioned Bethune's plan for a unified blood transfusion service. Laughing derisively, Bethune pulled out a huge wad of bills from his money belt and said, "Money talks, money talks." He said he was leaving for Valencia in the morning and that he felt certain he could bend the Sanidad Militar to his will through the assurance of Canadian financial support. However, a few minutes later, when Sise took him aside to say that Sorensen had learned that Durán i Jordà was putting up a spirited opposition to the idea of naming Bethune as chief of the proposed service, even Bethune's confidence must have been shaken.

Hazen Sise in the uniform
of the Instituto canadiense.
Photographer unknown.
(Library and Archives
Canada PA-172325)

On Monday morning Bethune arrived at the offices of the Sanidad Militar in Valencia. In the brief meeting that took place, Cerrada made it clear that the Sanidad Militar would not establish a unified service with him in command and that Bethune had also lost autonomous control over the Instituto in Madrid. Two of the Spanish doctors already working there would share responsibility with him in its operation. Durán i Jordà's objections and the escalating opposition to foreigners in any position of responsibility within the military structure were important obstacles to Bethune's plans, as was his inability to speak Spanish. However, after rejecting Bethune's proposal, Cerrada emphasized that the Sanidad Militar fully expected Canadian financial support for the Madrid unit to continue, in addition to the funds that Bethune had pledged for the new branch that he had proposed for Valencia. Money was, in fact, talking, but not in the way Bethune had hoped.

This rejection of his plans marked a turning point during Bethune's stay in Spain and had a profoundly disillusioning effect on his attitude and behaviour and his relationship with the Spanish military authorities. To Bethune, their response represented nothing more than blind bureaucracy preventing the creation of a desperately needed service that would save many lives. The fact that Cerrada had seemed to encourage his proposal in late January and had led him on for five more weeks before turning him down only deepened his resentment. From his arrival in November he had believed that he was involved in a revolutionary movement that had freed itself from various defects in bourgeois administrations. Now he was convinced that the administrators of the Republican government were no different from the bureaucrats he had known all his life in capitalist society. Feeling betrayed, he burned with anger.

Despite the bitterness that now consumed him, Bethune had to return at once to Madrid to give his full attention to the operation of the blood

Bethune returns to his vehicle after an attack near Guadalajara. (Attributed to Geza Kárpáthi. Roderick Stewart collection)

transfusion service. Through the last three weeks of February, the Spanish doctors of the Instituto had been frequently called into action, and although combat had ended before Bethune returned on March 2, a Republican casualty list of nearly 10,000 meant that the demand for blood continued.

Several days later another Nationalist assault on Madrid began, this time from north of the city. Acting in response to a call from the International Brigade hospital in Guadalajara on Friday March 12, Bethune set out in the Ford with ten bottles of blood and a refrigerator. With him were Sorensen, Geza Kárpáthi, and Antonio Culebras, one of the Spanish doctors in the Instituto. They had just passed the village of Torija when they ran into a long line of Republican solders in headlong retreat. Ignoring calls from his companions to turn around, Bethune continued driving until a bullet thudded into a front fender of the Ford. At this point, with bullets whistling by the vehicle, Bethune pulled to a halt and shouted, "Out, everybody out." Needing no orders, the others scrambled out; when the firing stopped they bent low to the ground and ran nearly 100 metres across an open field. Crouched beside the Ford before he followed the others, Bethune glanced up. In the middle of the windshield on the driver's side was a bullet hole. If he had remained in his seat a few seconds longer, he realized, he would have been killed. Shaken, he followed his companions to the wood. From there the four men made their way to Torija, where Bethune and Culebras worked for several hours in a casualty clearing station before they were taken back to Madrid in an army truck. The Ford was returned to the Instituto the next day. The following is Bethune's account of the visit to the hospital in Guadalajara.

The hospital stood at the top of the hill on the right as we crossed the bridge coming into the town of Guadalajara. It was about eleven – the clear, cold-bright day of March 12. In the Ford was Henning Sorensen, Geysa [Geza], and Calebras [Culebras], my Spanish assistant. I was driving. In the back we had a refrigerator and ten pint bottles of preserved blood packed in a wire basket. We had left Madrid at ten and had made the 54 kilometres in less than an hour, rolling along that fine paved Zaragosa road at well over seventy most of the time.

At Alcala de Henares we had looked for one of our hospitals but found they had moved over night up to the front, leaving behind, in their hurry, their refrigerator. We picked it up and were taking it to them.

All the roads showed the evidence of the battle ahead. We passed truck after truck loaded with young soldiers standing in the swaying cars with bayonets fixed, singing and shouting as we shot past. No more could be seen the old signs they used to paint on the side – no more C.N.T., U.G.T., F.A.I., C.P. – now just the great red five-pointed star of the people's united army.

Tanks ahead – a string of them – like great dinosaurs, you didn't realize until you tried to pass them how fast they were moving on their seeming-clumsy caterpillar wheels – 25, 30, 40, 45 miles an hour – we catch up and pass with a wave of our hand to the unseen driver. Gasoline trucks, bread wagons, donkey carts, mule trains all moving up. Yes, a drive was on. How important? Who are those steel helmeted troops – a shout in German – the famous Thaelmann Battalion going into action. It must be important. They are the feared "shock troops" of the International Brigade.

The wind was piercing cold as we crossed the plain. Blowing straight down from snow-covered peaks of the Guadarrama range on our left, glitter-ing so near, it made us turn up the collars of our warm brown coats and thank again, below our breath, the generous Syndicate of Tailors of Madrid who had presented us with them the week before. The front left window of the car was broken and had been for a week – hit by the swinging pole of a mule train – no time to lay the car up now for repairs.

Fifty, sixty, seventy, eighty kilometers an hour – God, what a swell road! At this rate we could be in Franco's line in half an hour's driving!

Sharp left turn at the top of the hill and there was the 500 bed hospital. No more red crosses now. Last week the fascist planes tried to bomb it so down came the cross – too easy a mark to hit – 500 wounded helpless men, too good a chance to miss.

The sure sign of an engagement were the long rows of blood-drenched stretchers, propped up on end, leaning against the walls, waiting to be washed.

All was bustle and hurry.

"Yes, go straight up." So up we go to the operating room. Here three tables are at work, the close air heavy with the fumes of ether. Casting a glance, a nod, a salud to the chief surgeon as we cross the room to the white

Bethune arriving at the Blood Hospital of Guadalajara. Geza Kárpáthi.
(Library and Archives Canada PA-116888)

enamelled refrigerator standing against the wall. The row of empty blood
bottles on the top tell the story – three, five, seven empties and inside, only
three unused.

"Better leave them six now; must come back tomorrow." "All right?" – the
chief surgeon looks up for a second from the table. Nods his head and smiles.

"Where are the tags?"

"Here," says a nurse and pulls a handful of blood-stained bottle tags from
her apron. A glance at each – on the back is written the name, the battalion,
the wound, the date of the recipient. "Let's go." Out of the door, down the
long corridor filled with stretcher-men, doctors, nurses and walking
wounded to Dr. Jolly's department. His fine, open New Zealand face breaks
into a smile as he sees us. We are old friends from early days in Madrid.

"Where's the refrigerator?"

"We have it in the car outside."

"Good, bring it in, we need it. There's a rush on."

The room is packed with wounded. They sit on the floor with blood-stained bandages on head, arms and legs, waiting to be dressed.

"Sorry, I must go now. Just operated on an Italian captain, poor fellow. Shot through the stomach. Hope he will live. André wants to see you. He's used up all his blood."

We feel fine. We feel like a successful salesman who has just placed a big order for goods. This is great! Isn't it grand to be needed, to be wanted!

So we bring the refrigerator in and set it down and plug in. Inside we put our remaining four bottles of blood. Here comes André, Jolly's assistant. A young French doctor just out of medical school, his fantastic black, short-cut beard making him look like a young pirate. He shakes our hand and bursts into rapid machine-gun French.

"Can you leave me another two needles? I need another syringe. I broke one last night. Can you give me some more grouping serums?"

"Sure." His thanks are effusive.

"I want to write my thesis for my master's degree in the University of Paris on blood transfusion at the front. Will you Canadians help me?"

"Sure." More effusions, more French. Dr. Jolly calls him from the operating room.

"I must go now, but there's a wounded man upstairs from the International Brigade and we can't make out what nationality he is. He can't speak English, French, Italian, Spanish or German. He's been hit by a bomb, lost one hand. We had to amputate the other and he's blinded in one eye. He needs a blood transfusion. We have to operate but I'm afraid he can't stand the shock. Will you give him a blood transfusion?"

"Let's go."

"Where's the man you can't make understand?" The pretty Spanish nurse shakes her dark head with a sad smile.

"Oh, there's lots of those."

"He's lost both hands and he's blind."

"Oh, I know, here, come, this ward."

Yes, it must be him. He's a big fellow with a great bloody bandage on his head. Must be six feet anyway, close to 200 lbs. His swollen face is covered with caked blood. Half an hour from the line. Still has his old shirt on. It's covered with stiff blood. Where hands used to be are two shapeless bundles of bloody bandages.

"Sorensen, come here."

At the name, the man turns his head slowly and from his swollen lips a question painfully comes. I can't understand, but Henning breaks into a rapid strange speech. "Why, he's Swedish. No wonder they can't understand him."

Yes, he needs a transfusion. Two tourniquets still in place to check the blood flow from both torn radial arteries. Must have lost a couple of quarts from the look of his face and feeble pulse. Five minutes and we're ready – blood heated to body temperature, grouped, syringe all sterilized. I look at the label "Blood number 695, Donor number 1106, Group IV, collected Madrid 6th March." Yes, it's O.K. No haemolysis. Let's go – needle in, syringe working smoothly – five minutes and it's finished.

Talking with a wounded soldier. (Hazen Sise. Library and Archives Canada PA-116905)

"Feel better?"

Translation. A twist from his bruised lips is his reply.

Henning bends over him with the anxious, distressed air of a father for his only child. They talk. I clean the syringe and pack the bag. Then back.

"What's the pulse?" Yes, one hundred and stronger, color better. He'll do.

"Come," to Sorensen. He tears himself away with reluctance, a backward glance at the door, a word, a reply.

"What did he say?"

Sorensen, quiet, mournful and low: "He said, 'ten days ago I was in Sweden. I have been in Spain three days. This was my first engagement, and now I am no more use to my comrades. I have done nothing for the cause.'

"Done nothing!" We look at each other with amazed eyes. "Done nothing!" What modesty, what courage, what a soul!

Yet that is the spirit of the International Brigade; of ten thousand determined unconquerable men, with no thought of themselves, with no thought of sacrifice, but simply and with a pure heart ready to lay down their lives for their friends. "Greater love hath no man more than this!"

These are your comrades in Spain.

To them – salud!

"With the Canadian Transfusion Unit at Guadalajara"
*Daily Clarion* [Toronto], 17 July 1937

# 8 ◆ UNRAVELLING

After the Battle of Guadalajara, Bethune was forced to deal with several problems that had been festering for some time in the Instituto. First was his relationship with the Spanish medical doctors, primarily Vicente Goyanes and Antonio Culebras, who in accordance with the orders of the Sanidad Militar had assumed joint control of the management of the renamed Instituto hispano-canadiense with Bethune. These two doctors had been students of Dr. Gustavo Pittaluga, a professor at the University of Madrid and the organizer of the city's first blood transfusion unit, which began operating on the third day of the uprising in July 1936. In early January 1937, the Madrid Defence Council had ordered Goyanes and Culebras to join the staff of the Instituto. Two more doctors, Valentin de la Loma and Andrés Sanz Vilaplana, arrived in early February.

For the first five days after Bethune left Madrid on January 11 to buy the Renault, he had left Sise in control, but after Bethune summoned him to Barcelona, Sise remained away for a full month. During that time Kajsa Rothman was nominally in charge. The thirty-three-year-old Rothman, a tall, compellingly attractive Swede, had arrived in Barcelona before the military uprising. The first Swede to volunteer for the Republican cause, she was immediately incorporated into a militia unit, and when women were withdrawn from the front, she served as a nurse. From the beginning she was unreservedly involved. Repeatedly returning to Sweden to raise

Sise and Bethune. Photographer unknown. (Library and Archives Canada PA-117454)

Kajsa Rothman. (Reproduced
by permission of the Labour
Movement Archives and Library,
Stockholm)

funds, holding rallies, and writing articles for the liberal Swedish newspaper, the *Karlstad-Tidningen*, she made herself a source of information
and was an inspiration to Swedish volunteers. In late December, Bethune
had invited her to move into the Instituto, ostensibly for the purpose of
acting as his secretary. She performed rather well in that capacity and also
became Bethune's lover. Able to speak Spanish, she kept the administration of the Instituto functioning while Bethune, Sise, and Sorensen were
away. Irritated by the way she swaggered about in her militiaman uniform
and Sam Browne belt, Goyanes and Culebras were unwilling to be responsible to someone who was not only another foreigner but a woman, and
Bethune's lover in the bargain.

They were also deeply concerned with questions of salary and rank.
Goyanes, who had an army rank of lieutenant, had come to the Instituto
with the understanding that he would be promoted to captain. Culebras
expected to be granted the same rank. Bethune had promised in late
January to pay Culebras a captain's salary and to make up the difference

between what Goyanes was receiving in army pay as a lieutenant and the salary of captain. Unfortunately, Bethune's involvement in the Málaga–Almería tragedy had delayed his departure for Paris to collect the money that had been wired to him from Toronto; this meant that the Spaniards had worked throughout February without pay. When Bethune reached Madrid on March 2, he paid the back salaries of Culebras and Goyanes and also those of the newly appointed doctors, Valentin de la Loma and Andrés Sanz Vilaplana. As to rank, when Bethune was finally forced to admit that the Sanidad Militar had rejected his proposal, it was apparent that his promise to arrange for the promotion of Goyanes and Culebras had come to nothing.

However, the problems in the Instituto ran deeper than these resentments. Sise had told Bethune that on his return to Madrid from Almería on February 17 he found the doctors in a hostile, almost rebellious, mood, openly critical of Bethune's prolonged absence. There was even the suggestion that because Bethune was not a hematologist they doubted his competence to head the unit.

On his return, Bethune picked up on all this. The atmosphere of the Instituto was markedly different from the cheerful bustle that had characterized the early days of its existence. The élan was gone, and government red tape was reducing efficiency. The exasperation caused by what he considered to be continuous, absurd, and unnecessary hindrances to the running of the Instituto began to affect his self-control, and on occasion he gave way to outbursts of rage, some of them violent. In one fit of temper, he picked up a chair and smashed it against a wall. But it was the attitude of some of the doctors that bothered him most. They showed no enthusiasm for their work, which apparently they considered as nothing more than a job. Growing increasingly impatient, Bethune began to accuse them of being "bourgeois loafers." The problem with Culebras went deeper. After Culebras arrived at the Instituto, Bethune agreed to hire his wife Manolita and three other people. Only later did he learn that they were Culebras' sister, her fiancé, and Culebras' brother's fiancée. In a staff of fifteen Spaniards, they constituted a powerful faction that acted in solidarity when conflicts with the others arose. In addition, Culebras and Loma were feuding. These internecine struggles poisoned the work atmosphere and reduced efficiency.

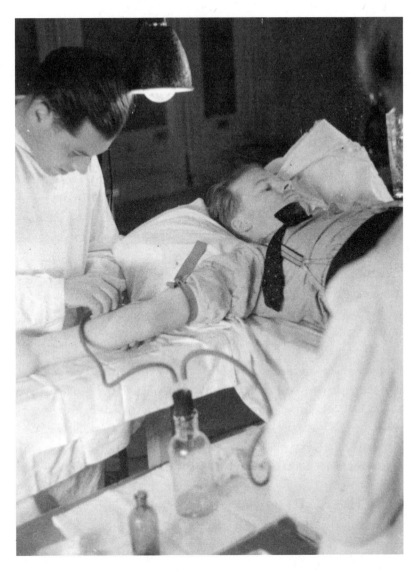

Dr. Culebras, assisted by the Canadian journalist Jean Watts, extracts blood from Allen May. (Hazen Sise. Library and Archives Canada PA-117450)

The imposed restructuring of the Instituto and the indolence of the doctors caused Bethune to fear that the vigorous spirit of the early days would be lost. He worried that the Instituto would become ineffective, soulless, and paralyzed by inertia. Nevertheless, he softened his tone considerably for CASD reading when he wrote the following letter to Benjamin Spence on March 9:

Dear Ben:

If you have received all my cables sent within the last three weeks along with the one sent by May from Valencia you will be fairly well posted on developments to date.

This letter is an attempted review of all your cables, in which I will try to answer your questions just as they come before me.

Regarding the sketchiness of correspondence: you must have realized by now that the amount of work I am obliged to do here leaves me very little time for letter writing. The Spanish doctors who work with us seem to be incapable of accepting responsibility or acting on their own initiative. Consequently, I am forced to attend to every detail myself. Then, there has been a 200% increase in work. From a happy little company of three we have grown into a large organization – predominantly Spanish and all hope of quietness or peace has vanished. However, Allen May has been appointed official secretary and he will attend to correspondence from now on.

There is no chance of placing more Canadians here at present. The Spanish trade unions are jealous of their rights and insist that only union chauffeurs be permitted to drive Government cars. One [of] the chiefs of the Sanidad Militar was arrested recently for driving the car which had been given to him to use. Now he has two chauffeurs and can move when, and if, the chauffeurs are willing.

We could use another Canadian doctor but he must be able to speak either French or Spanish and preferably both. Otherwise he would be almost useless. That of course, does not mean the other Canadian doctors and nurses could not be sent to other units. There is still a great need of trained nurses and English-speaking doctors and I am sure that anyone who wants to come here can find work on the fronts.

When we were at the American hospital a few days ago Dr. Barsky agreed that a brain surgeon would be tremendously valuable. Such a man would have to be accompanied by his own anesthetist and assistant and a complete set of brain instruments.

Another project which the committee might investigate is the possibility of sending a Canadian dental truck. Dentists and dental facilities are absolutely non-existent on the fronts and there is a crying need for them. The cost of equipping a complete travelling dental clinic in, say, a Dodge Truck,

Bethune beside the Renault. (Hazen Sise. Library and Archives
Canada PA-172601)

with a workshop, X-ray and laboratory, would [be] about $10,000. An appeal
to the Canadian Dental Association should receive a favorable response.
The truck should carry a staff of three – dentist, technician and chauffeur.

Re: the two men who wish to come here. Mercier could be used in the
International Brigade where he would receive militiaman's pay.

You did not give me any indication of Hommelfarb's [sic] technical quali-
fications so I would suggest that he be sent as an ambulance driver to Dr.
Neuman, chief medical officer of the International brigade, at Albacete.
Unless he is sent as an ambulance driver he will not be able to get across

the border and it would be advisable, in his accompanying letter, not to mention the International Brigade.

Our unit is not broadcasting at present. The work has been taken over entirely by a new bureau which is being formed by Ted Allan, Jean Watts and Herbert Kline, editor of New Theatre. I would be glad to commence broadcasting again when the organization of our work begins to function more smoothly. When that time will come [is] impossible to say but if it does I will send you a cable so that you can prepare for reception in Canada.

Re: food. There is a definite shortage of food and only two ways of getting it into the country. One is by rail through France. The other is in ships under British or American registry. Ships under the flags of these two countries would have an uninterrupted passage and I strongly urge again my repeated suggestion of the practicability of chartering a Canadian ship under British registry, filling it full of food and sending it directly into the port of Valencia. You could send some children's clothing. But it must be new. Second-hand clothing is not to be considered.

Our experiment with electrical refrigeration in the truck, depending on batteries and a dynamo, proved unsatisfactory. It is true that we were able to transport blood for distances of 1,000 miles and use it at the end of that distance, but the system broke down when the rough roads damaged the dynamo which is used to charge the batteries. As a result of our trip to Almería I have sent the truck into France with Hazen Sise to have it fitted out with a supply of Butane gas. This gas is stored in small cylinders which reduces the weight carried by the truck by at least 100%. It provides a continual supply of gas with which to run the Electrolux refrigerator and as it is a simple technique our worries about an electrical refrigeration system for the summer should be over.

In the last week we have placed nine Electrolux refrigerators in hospitals on the Madrid front. In the coming week we expect to place six more in casualty clearing stations. The area in which we operate now extends over a radius of 150 kilometers and it is our intention to equip every hospital in that territory, that requires blood, with a refrigerator in which to keep their supplies in good condition. In actual transfusions made in the last month there has been an increase of 300% and we expect a proportional increase in March.

In the cable that reached me in Paris there was a confusion in the name of Allen May. We thought it read "Allen May Youn." However it was an error quickly rectified.

We met in Paris and between us we sent out over 100 posters to you and Norman Lee in Montreal. If you have not received them it must be the fault of the censors either in France or Spain, or the Customs in Canada. It is practically impossible to send Spanish souvenirs for display out to you. However we have placed you on the mailing lists of the bureaus of propaganda in Barcelona and Valencia and their work is to send such material to other countries.

The question of Spanish delegates must be taken up with the Department of Propaganda of Valencia. It is impossible to arrange here, we have discovered. In Paris we tried but could get no satisfaction because they had difficulty in understanding why we needed Spanish workers who could speak English. Such a thing was impossible, they said, and naturally, they could not understand why we should ask the impossible.

Re: your letter of January 14. Several tons of preserved meats, canned milk, butter, bacon, canned vegetables, potatoes and especially flour, are urgently required. These should be sent directly to me in Madrid for distribution to our donors.

Re: letter of February 9. Allen May is with us and is now the official secretary of the unit. He will be extremely valuable in his capacity of publicity agent and connecting link between our work here and the Committee in Canada. In his spare time, if he has any, he will drive as a chauffeur. I am glad he is here because the combination of my laziness, bad writing and overwork made correspondence an almost impossible task. I cannot place Norman McLeod now but the time may come, shortly, when I can use him.

As I wrote you from Paris, I have suggested to the Spanish Government that a Children's City should be erected with the assistance of international finances. However, it is strongly advisable that this suggestion should not come from me but from the Spanish Government. We discussed the project with architects in Barcelona and they were quite enthusiastic. Now the matter lies with the Barcelona Government. Officialdom there may create obstacles but I still feel that the plan has wonderful possibilities.

The Spanish Government now considers that the workers of Canada are responsible for the maintenance of the blood transfusion service during the duration of this war. We must not fail them.

Salud

NB

Bethune to Benjamin Spence<br>
Province of Ontario Archives<br>
Albert Alexander MacLeod fonds F126, MU 7590, file 12

After Bethune's return to Madrid, the dislike that he and Culebras felt for one another became overt. Neither Loma nor Sanz shared Culebras' loathing of Bethune, but both sympathized with his unwillingness to serve under a foreigner. Culebras resented his subservient role and felt that he should replace Bethune as *comandante* of the Instituto. As a member of the Communist Party he had some influence, and there is little doubt that he had provided to the Sanidad Militar information designed to undermine Bethune. To him, it was sweet justice that he was now able to share with Goyanes a degree of control over Bethune. To Bethune, on the other hand, it was intolerable to share power in the management of the Instituto with a man whom he despised and considered a slacker. This situation also intensified his contempt for the judgement of the Sanidad Militar.

From the point of view of the Spanish, the behaviour of the Canadians also left much to be desired. Many years later, Manolita Culebras wrote of them: "They took up space, they ate, they gossiped, they smoked and they drank up to the point that when there was no more whiskey that they had sent from the United States, they drank the laboratory alcohol." It is highly unlikely that the Canadians actually drank the laboratory alcohol, however thirsty they were. The accusation, no doubt, stems from the intense dislike of Bethune felt by members of the Culebras family. The reference to drinking, however, is accurate. Bethune in particular always drank a good deal, and much more when he was upset.

Not only was Bethune now drinking heavily, but he was also not eating properly. Because of the severe food shortage, the menu offered by the cook at the Instituto seldom varied from beans, lentils, the occasional piece of fish and, rarely, meat. Bethune now went for days eating only black bread and drinking black coffee. Another problem was his recurrent

In a classroom of the Ciudad Universitaria (University of Madrid).
(Attributed to Hazen Sise. Roderick Stewart collection)

insomnia. Often unable to sleep at night, he found it impossible to maintain the practice he had begun at Trudeau Sanatorium of having an afternoon rest. This had been a problem from the early days of the blood transfusion service; his response whenever exhaustion overcame him had been to lie down wherever he was and instantly fall asleep. Invariably, no more than an hour later he would awaken, revived and eager to go on. Now he no longer had such resilience. Excessive drinking, improper diet, and lack of sleep all contributed to his increasingly frequent outbursts of violent temper.

The Spaniards and Canadians alike became deeply concerned by the change in Bethune's behaviour. Two of the Canadians were so alarmed that they decided to take concrete action. One of them, Ted Allan, was the newest member of the unit. A twenty-one-year-old writer from Montreal, Allan had left his job as a reporter on the staff of the Communist paper the *Daily Clarion* to come to Spain in February to join the International Brigades. When Peter Kerrigan, the political commissar of the British

Brigade, learned from Allan that he had met Bethune in Montreal, he sent him to Madrid. Having heard rumours of difficulties in the Instituto, Kerrigan gave Allan the assignment of ferreting out information on Bethune's performance. Bethune liked Allan, invited him to join the growing ranks of the Instituto, and – partly in jest – named him political commissar of the blood transfusion service.

The other Canadian concerned about Bethune's behaviour was Henning Sorensen, whose disillusionment had been building for some time. He had felt privileged to be Bethune's interpreter. But he took an instant dislike to Kajsa Rothman and was upset when she began to act as interpreter whenever she and Bethune were together. Extremely sensitive and easily hurt, Sorensen was jealous. He began to turn against Bethune. He could not accept that, as a dedicated Party member, Bethune allowed his personal interests, especially bourgeois diversions such as sex and drinking to excess, to interfere with his commitment to the cause. Finally, he reached the conclusion that Bethune was not performing as a loyal Party member and must be replaced.

While Sorensen was pondering what action to take, matters came to a head. Apparently because of his total disaffection with the Sanidad Militar, which he believed had broken its promises to him, Bethune had not sent the money he had pledged to establish a transfusion service in Valencia. When Colonel Cerrada sent a request to Bethune for the promised funds, Sorensen, who translated Cerrada's message, urged him to comply, but Bethune became infuriated and refused.

This event, which occurred just after he had learned from Ted Allan why he had come to the Instituto, encouraged Sorensen to decide that some check had to be imposed on Bethune. Together he and Allan decided to send a report of their criticism of Bethune's conduct via the Spanish Communist party to Tim Buck, Secretary of the Canadian Communist party. This action may have emboldened Sorensen to confront Bethune on another long-simmering grievance, the role of Kajsa Rothman in the Instituto. He presented Bethune with an ultimatum: unless he evicted her, Sorensen would leave the Instituto. When Bethune refused, Sorensen left Madrid on March 19 for Valencia, where, with the assistance of Dr. Juan Planelles, Medical Director of the Fifth Regiment in Madrid, he was given a position in the Sanidad Militar.

A week later, after Bethune had ignored two telegrams ordering him to report to the headquarters of the Sanidad Militar, he received a third informing him that failure to comply with the order would lead to his arrest. Bethune left Madrid on April 1 for Valencia. The next day, when he entered Cerrada's office, Bethune was surprised to find Sorensen waiting there to act as interpreter. The meeting consisted of a series of hostile exchanges between Cerrada and Bethune in which Sorensen was forced to soften Bethune's biting remarks. After referring to several examples of Bethune's deportment that he regarded as undesirable, Cerrada concluded, "We don't understand your behaviour, considering you are a Communist." Bethune suddenly changed tack. Lowering his voice, he explained that their differences resulted from various factors: his failure to receive all the messages sent to him; his total involvement during the aftermath of the Battle of Guadalajara, as well as the ever-present problem of the language barrier. "It was," he insisted, "all a misunderstanding." The encounter ended, despite the failure to resolve the central issue, with a cooling of tempers.

This close call snapped Bethune into the realization that he was losing control of the situation. To the Sanidad Militar's decision to take command of the Instituto was added the growing hostility between him and Culebras, who seemed to be taking advantage of the circumstances. But Bethune was reluctant to leave the service he had brought into being with so much daring, imagination, and effort. He was convinced that, without him, the Instituto would become no more than an ordinary health unit – bureaucratized, less and less active, and less Canadian.

Bethune returned to Madrid immediately after the meeting with Cerrada. Before following him, Sorensen remained to provide information to the military police for a report that they would later make on the history of the activities of Bethune and the operation of the blood transfusion service. The report would include, among other things, the absurd suggestion that Bethune and Kajsa Rothman may have been acting as Nationalist spies.

Back in Madrid on Tuesday, Sorensen informed Sise and Allen May that the reorganization of the Sanidad Militar, which would end the autonomy of all foreign units, would be announced later in the week. He pointed out that, although they would no longer have a say in the operation of the Instituto, if they still wanted Canadian financial aid they should try to persuade Bethune to return to Canada to engage in publicity to maintain the flow of funds to Spain.

After many hours of discussion, the three of them convinced Bethune that he would be most useful to the Spanish cause by returning to Canada with the film *Heart of Spain* that Geza Kárpáthi and an American writer, Herbert Kline, were on the verge of completing. He finally agreed to their plan. However, for the next six days Bethune pondered the promise he had made. Then, on Monday, April 12, without consulting his comrades, he sent the following cable to the CASD:

Government decrees all organizations in Spain whether Spanish or Foreign must come under control of Ministry of War. No independent organizations allowed. The Sanidad Militar have taken over control [of] Canadian Unit. Our positions now nominal. Fortunately transfusion service is well established and can carry on without us. Ninety percent capital equipment expenditure paid out. Strongly urge you act immediately. Authorize me by cable as Chief to first withdraw Canadian personnel, second hand over to Government refrigerators and equipment, third agree to provide two hundred dollars monthly six months for maintenance [of] institute, fourth return Canada with such Canadians as desire with film for antifascist propaganda. Our work as Canadians here is finished. Remember Kleber and the International Column. Only future cables signed Beth Bethune are from me. Continue collection funds. Many schemes more urgent now than Blood Transfusion. Will inform you later. Salud.

Library and Archives Canada<br>Ted Allan fonds, MG30-D388 Volume 16, File 3

Totally unprepared for Bethune's suggestion to bring to an abrupt end the Canadian role in the operation of the blood transfusion service, Chairman Benjamin Spence and other members of the CASD wanted more information. When Spence immediately replied with a request for the opinions of other members of the unit, he received no answer. On Friday, Spence sent a cable addressed to "Bethunit" asking for a reply. On Saturday Bethune cabled back: "Awaiting government decision reor-

Bethune writing. (Hazen Sise. Roderick Stewart collection)

ganization next few days. Till then no fresh news. Salud." Two days later he sent the following letter addressed to the "Jefe de Sanidad Militar":

Camarada:

In view of the fact that the Instituto Hispano-Canadiense de Transfusion de Sangre as conceived by me in January is now operating as an efficient, well-organized institute, and as part of the Sanidad Militar, it is clear to me that my function as chief of the organization here in Spain has come to a natural end. Since I am firmly of the opinion that all services of the Republican Army should be controlled by the Spanish people I hereby offer my resignation as chief of the organization.

If the resignation is accepted I will at once proceed to Canada to carry out propaganda work in connection with the Institute in support of the Popular Front.

In view of the necessity of the continuation of financial support of the
Institute in Spain from the Popular Front in Canada I hereby delegate my
authority as Chief representative of the Canadian Committee to Aid Spanish
Democracy to the following members: Allen May, Ted Allan, Hazen Sise and
Henning Sorensen. I would also suggest that the functions of the above
members of the Committee should be as follows: Allen May, official secretary
and responsible of the Canadian Committee; Ted Allan, political commissar;
Hazen Sise, director of transport; Henning Sorensen, liaison officer between
Canadian representatives and Sanidad Militar.

Also, in view of the urgency of the situation and the necessity of showing
our propaganda film as quickly as possible, I would like my resignation to
take effect immediately.

Dr. Norman Bethune

Library and Archives Canada
Ted Allan fonds, MG30 D388 Volume 16, File 3

After posting the letter, Bethune showed a copy to his comrades. An-
gered by Bethune's unilateral action, and realizing that officials in the
Sanidad Militar would want a detailed explanation, Sorensen, Sise, and
May left for Valencia. On their return, they held lengthy discussions with
Bethune, and on May 4 he joined them in sending a cable to the CASD
stating that the unit should continue functioning under Spanish control
and that he would return to Canada with the film to raise money.

The rapid unfolding of events during those hectic days imposed an
almost unbearable emotional strain on the Canadians in the unit.
Bethune, however, appeared strangely calm. Although he was often irri-
table and hot-tempered, he was also capable of becoming lost in thought,
distancing himself emotionally from his surroundings even during
periods of great confusion and frenetic activity. Now he seemed curiously
indifferent to the turmoil he had created, and became absorbed in pondering the ideological fundamentals that had recently changed the course
of his life. After announcing that he would return to Canada, he wrote a
long letter setting out his thoughts on the role of the artist in society. A
few Canadian friends received copies of this document written under such

extraordinary circumstances. It was later published under the title *An Apology for Not Writing Letters.*

This is an attempt at an explanation why I, who think of you so often, with love and affection, have not written – or so briefly – since my arrival in Spain.

I had thought to say simply (that is, shortly) – I have been too busy; I am a man of action; I have no time to write. Yet as I look at these words, I see they are false. They simply aren't true. In fact, I have had plenty of time to write you, that is if I had cared to write, but, in truth, I did not care. Now why is this? Why have I not written to those of you who, I know, without illusion, would like to hear from me? Why is it I can not put down one word after another on paper and make a letter out of them?

I will try and be truthful. It is difficult to be truthful, isn't it?

First of all, I don't feel like writing. I don't feel the necessity of communication. I don't feel strongly the necessity of a re-construction of experience – my actions and the actions of others – into the form of art which a letter should take. As an artist, unless that re-construction take a satisfactory form which is truthful, simple and moving, I will not, nay, I can not, write at all. I feel that unless I can re-construct those remembrances of action into reality for you, I will not attempt it. To me, a letter is an important thing – words are important things. At present, I don't feel any necessity to communicate these experiences. They are in me, have changed me, but I don't want to talk about them. I don't want to talk about them yet.

Besides, I am afraid to write you. I am afraid of the banality of words, of the vocal, the verbal, of the literary re-construction. I am afraid they won't be true.

Only by a shared physical experience – tactile, visual or auditory – may an approximately similar emotion be felt by two people without the aid of art. Only through art, can the truth of a non-shared experience be transmitted. To share with you what I have seen, what I have experienced in the past six months, is impossible without art. Without art, experience becomes, on the one hand, the denuded, bare bones of fact, – a static, still-life, – the how-many-ness of things; or, on the other hand, the swollen, exaggerated shapes of fantastically-coloured romanticism. And I will do neither. I refuse to write either way. Both are false – the first by its poverty, the second by its excess.

Bethune with nurses and members of the International Brigades. (Attributed to Hazen Sise. National Film Board of Canada)

So I despair of my ability to transpose the reality of experience into the reality of the written word. Art should be the legitimate and recognizable child of experience. I am afraid of a changeling. I am afraid it would have none of the unmistakable inherited characteristics of its original, true, parental reality.

I can not write you, my friends, because this art of letters is a second, a repeated form of action. And one form of action at a time is enough. I can not do both – but successively, with an interval of a year, or ten years. Perhaps I can do both. I don't know. I don't think it matters very much.

I think that art has no excuse, no reason for existence except through the re-creation – by a dialectical process – of a new form of reality, for the old experience – transmitted through a man's sensorium – changed and illuminated by his conscious and unconscious mind. Exact reproduction is useless –

that way lies death. The process of change from the old to the new is not a flat circular movement – a turn and return on itself, but helical and ascending.

The process of creative art is the negation of the negation. First there is the change, that is, the negation, of the original, the positive reality; then the second change (or negation), which is a re-affirmation, a re-birth, through art, of the original experience, to the new positive, the new form of reality.

Let us take an example from painting – a moving object such as a tree swaying in the wind, a child at play, a bird in flight – any form of action, seen and perceived. This is the positive, the thesis. Reduced from the dynamic positive in time and space to a static form, by representation, (in this case, by paint on canvas) it becomes the negation of action, the denial of action. This is the antithesis. Then by the miracle of creative art, this static thing, (of necessity static, owing, to the medium employed) is vivified, transformed into movement again, into life again, but into a new life, becomes positive again, becomes the negation of the negation of the negation, the synthesis – the union of life and death, of action and non-action, the emergence of the new from the old within the new.

Now the same thing applies to the literary art, the plastic arts, music, the dance or what not – any art form. And unless that fresh emergent form, with its core of the old, is a new thing, a dynamic thing, a quick and living thing, it is not art. It arouses no response except intellectual appreciation, the facile response to familiar, recognizable objects, or admiration for technical skill.

And because I can't write you, my friends, as I should like to write you, because my words are poor, anaemic and hobbling things, I have not written. Yes, I could write, but I am ashamed to write – like this:

"We were heavily shelled today. It was very uncomfortable. Fifty people were killed in the streets. The weather is lovely now although the winter has been hard. I am well. I think of you often. Yes, it is true I love you. Good bye."

I put them down and look at these words with horror and disgust. I wish I could describe to you how much I dislike these words. "Uncomfortable" – good God! what a word to describe the paralyzing fear that seizes one when a shell bursts with a great roar and crash near by; "killed", for these poor huddled bodies of rags and blood, lying in such strange shapes, face down on the cobble-stones, or with sightless eyes upturned to a cruel and indifferent sky;

"lovely" when the sun falls on our numbed faces like a benediction; "well" when to be alive is well enough; "think" for that cry rising from our hearts day by day for remembered ones; "love" for this ache of separation.

So you see, it's no good.

Forgive me if I talk more about art. It must seem to you that I know either a great deal about it or nothing at all. I really know very little about it. I think it is very mysterious, very strange. But it seems to me to be a natural product of the subconscious mind of man, of all men, in some degree. Arising into the realm of deliberate thought, its life is imperilled. A theory of art reminds me of a medieval chart of the then-known world – curious, fantastic and wonderfully untrue. A theory of art is an attempt of the rational mind to impose its discipline and its order on the seeming chaos and seeming disorder of the emotional subconscious. If this is attempted – and it has frequently been attempted, a certain form of art, ordered and neat, arises. By its subjection to the conscious mind, to the deliberate directional thought of the artist and his theory, it lives for a while and then languishes and dies. It can not survive its separation from the great breeding ground of the unconscious. The mind (that alien in the attic) by its dictatorship, destroys the very thing it has discovered.

Most great artists of the world have been, – thank Heaven – "stupid" in the worldly sense. They didn't think too much, they simply painted. Driven on by an irresistable internal compulsion, they painted as they did, as they must paint.

A great artist lets himself go. He is natural. He "swims easily in the stream of his own temperament." He listens to himself. He respects himself. He has a deeper fund of strength to draw from than that arising from rational and logical knowledge. Yet how beautifully the dialectical process comes in again, – modified by thought, his primitive unconsciousness, conditioned by experience, reacts to reality and produces new forms of that reality. These particular forms of art arise, satisfy for their time, decay and die. But, by their appearance, they modify and influence succeeding art forms. They also modify and influence the very reality which produced them. Art itself never dies. Art itself is a great ever-blooming tree, timeless, indestructible and immortal. The particular art forms of a generation are the flowers of that immortal tree. They are the expressions of their particular time but they are the products also of all the preceding time.

The artist needs, among other things, leisure, immense quietness, privacy and aloneness. The environment in which he has his being, are those dark, sunless, yet strangely illuminated depths of the world's subconscious, – the warm, pulsating yet quiet depths of the other-world.

He comes up into the light of every-day, like a great leviathan of the deep, breaking the smooth surface of accepted things, gay, serious, sportive and destructive. In the bright banal glare of day, he enjoys the purification of violence, the catharsis of action. His appetite for life is enormous. He enters eagerly into the life of man, of all men. He becomes all men in himself. He views the world with an all-embracing eye which looks upwards, outwards, inwards and downwards, – understanding, critical, tender and severe. Then he plunges back once more, back into the depths of that other-world, – strange, mysterious, secret and alone. And there, in those depths, he gives birth to the children of his being – new forms, new colors, new sounds, new

Sorensen (at back, looking right) and Bethune with soldiers. (Hazen Sise. Roderick Stewart collection)

movements, reminiscent of the known, yet not the known, alike and yet unlike; strange yet familiar, calm, profound and sure.

The function of the artist is to disturb. His duty is to arouse the sleeper, to shake the complacent pillars of the world. He reminds the world of its dark ancestry, shows the world its present, and points the way to its new birth. He is at once the product and the preceptor of his time. After his passage we are troubled and made unsure of our too-easily accepted realities. He makes uneasy the static, the set and the still. In a world terrified of change, he preaches revolution – the principle of life. He is an agitator, a disturber of the peace – quick, impatient, positive, restless and disquieting. He is the creative spirit of life working in the soul of man.

But enough. Perhaps the true reason I can not write is that I'm too tired – another 150 miles on the road today, and what roads!

Our first job is to defeat fascism – the enemy of the creative artist. After that we can write about it.

Good bye. I do think of you with love and affection. Forgive me when I do not write.

Salud

Norman Bethune

> Research file for documentary film *Bethune* (1964)
> National Film Board Library, Montreal

Concerned about the failure of other members of the unit to respond to the request for their opinions, and suspicious that the situation in the unit was more serious than they had been led to believe, the CASD decided to send one of their members, A.A. MacLeod, to investigate and to persuade Bethune to return home as soon as possible. Spence sent a cable to Madrid stating the committee's decision and asking Bethune to take Sorensen with him to meet MacLeod in Paris on May 24. Certain that the reason Spence wanted Sorensen to accompany him to Paris was to allow MacLeod to learn his version of the events of the last few months, Bethune left Madrid alone on May 16. It was his definitive *adios* to Spain. He would never return.

For the next week he sought diversion in Paris by shopping, sightseeing, and attending the French national tennis championships. When

Photo montage of the Canadian members of the Instituto canadiense.
(Hazen Sise. Library and Archives Canada PA-114782)

Bethune met MacLeod on May 26, he made the focus of their discussions his project for the Children's City. Arguing that the Madrid unit would shortly fall under complete Spanish control, but not informing him that the Spaniards expected to continue receiving Canadian financial support for its maintenance, Bethune convinced MacLeod that a new appeal should be made in Canada for funds, but from now on it would be for the support of Spanish war orphans. He and MacLeod next presented the proposal to a Basque committee in Paris, who reacted enthusiastically and urged MacLeod and Bethune to fly to Bilbao to discuss the matter with Republican officials there.

On May 27 MacLeod cabled the CASD, informing them of his intention to fly to Bilbao with Bethune, after which he would go to Madrid to investigate the situation there. The CASD immediately replied that investigating the relationship between the Canadians and the Sanidad Militar and the immediate return of Bethune were far more pressing matters than the question of a method of caring for war orphans.

On May 31 MacLeod sent another cable to the CASD, asking them to accept responsibility for supporting 500 Spanish war orphans and suggesting that he go directly to Madrid to formally transfer the unit to the Sanidad Militar. He added that because of complications regarding putting the finishing touches on the film *The Heart of Spain,* Bethune could not yet sail for Canada. The CASD replied that it would consider the matter of support for war orphans, but that the most urgent matter for them was the immediate return of Bethune to begin a speaking tour across Canada. MacLeod told Bethune he had no choice but to leave on the first available ship.

# 9    ◆   THE RETURN

On June 2, Bethune, Geza Kárpáthi and Herbert Kline, carrying the unfinished film in their luggage, boarded the *Queen Mary* for New York. On their arrival on June 7, Bethune was greeted by several reporters. The following is the account of an interview with him conducted by L.S.B. Shapiro:

New York, June 7 – "What's the matter with England, France, the United States, Canada? Are they afraid that by supplying arms to the Loyalist forces they'll start a world war? Why, the world war has started. In fact, it's in its third stage – Manchuria, Ethiopia and now Spain. It's democracy against Fascism."

The speaker was Dr. Norman Bethune, Montreal physician who was head of the blood transfusion service on the Madrid front. His thin face was flushed; his lean body quivered and he pounded his fist in emphasis as he fairly shouted the words. Then he paused slightly to recover his composure.

"We in Madrid cannot understand such timidity, such poltroonery on the part of the democratic nations. Supplied with the proper arms, the Loyalists would throw the Franco forces into the sea in one month. The war would be over; the danger gone. But as long as Italy and Germany are openly waging war against the Spanish people, the war will go on indefinitely. And although the Fascists will never take Madrid and they'll never take Bilbao, the lingering Spanish war will surely spread all over the world."

The Montreal physician, who went to Spain seven months ago to take over the transfusion service with the assistance of Hazen Sise and Henning Sorenson [sic], of Montreal, and Allan [sic] May, of Toronto, arrived here today in the Queen Mary, travelling steerage.

(As quoted by The Canadian Press, Dr. Bethune said: "I wasn't spending the unit's money on first class tickets.")

Accompanied by two photographers who took action pictures on the Spanish war front, he will tour Canada for a brief period before returning to his duties in Madrid.

The tour will start in Toronto next Monday evening, and Dr. Bethune will appear in Montreal on Thursday, June 17. He will spend this week in New York, developing and cutting the films.

Although he spoke highly of the service of his companions, Sise, May and Sorenson [sic], and of the 21 Spanish doctors who make up his transfusion unit, Dr. Bethune waved aside any stories of personal heroism.

"Heroism is taken for granted in Loyalist Spain," he said. "The Spanish fighters have my completest admiration. You just can't break the spirit of the people no matter how intense the bombardment of Madrid. Great deeds are routine affairs. Why, one American in the Abraham Lincoln Battalion was wounded six times, and each time insisted on returning to the front. That is an ordinary case, but it is indicative of the spirit of the people.

"I'll tell you this. The rebels will never win Spain. The Loyalists will never agree to a truce. No, not until the last man, woman and child has been killed. They realize they are fighting the fight of democracy against Fascism."

Here the grim-faced, grey-haired physician again drew himself to his full height and pounded the words home.

"But they cannot understand, they cannot conceive it: to them it is unbelievable that the great democracies should declare neutrality laws which work against a legally-elected government fighting against rebels and foreign invaders.

"Do you think," and he lowered his voice in a confidential tone, "that Germany and Italy are fighting in Spain because they are against Bolshevism?

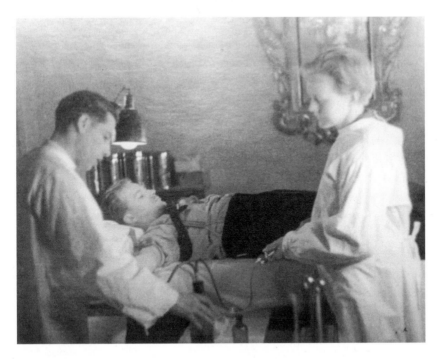

Dr. Culebras, Allen May, and Jean Watts. (Attributed to Hazen Sise. Roderick Stewart collection)

That is silly. The Communist party is a minor party in Spain. There is no Communist threat. Why, Negrin, the Premier, is a Right Republican. There are only two communists in the Government. There are not more than 250,000 Communists in all Spain.

"No, what Italy is fighting for is a strategic position in the Mediterranean. What Germany is fighting for are iron and manganese mines. They are the rebels. Franco is nothing. The German General Staff is directing the war and there are 100,000 Italians fighting. Why, oh why, can't the democratic nations see this? That's what the Spanish people cannot understand."

The physician stopped and shook his head as though he, too, were confused by the problems which confound the Spanish people.

"Until Russia sent arms," he continued, "the Spaniards were actually fighting with fists, with knives, with scythes. But Russia's help is not enough. We are getting nothing from France, nothing from Britain, nothing from Canada, nothing from America."

Your reporter broke in with a question. "If we take for granted that Germany and Italy are fighting for their own national motives," was the query, "what will Russia's price be in the case of a Loyalist victory?"

The answer came quickly.

"Naturally Russia is anxious to help in any anti-Fascist battle. But their price? Why, they are being paid on the line for every piece of equipment sent. Spain asks nothing except the right to buy arms freely for her rightful fight against rebels and invaders."

Dr. Bethune recalled the razing of Guernica and the retreat from Málaga. He was on the road from Málaga as thousands of Spanish families struggled along the highway in order to remain in Loyalist territory. He spoke spiritedly of the shelling of Almería, and the artillery warfare against Madrid, which he said was of no strategic value.

"They are getting away with murder. Simply murder," he said grimly. Dr. Bethune estimated that there are 250 Canadians fighting for the Loyalists. He is certain that there are none on the rebel side.

"And most of the Canadians are French-Canadian Catholics," he added. "There is no religious war in Madrid. The Lutheran Church is open every day. I attended services there every Sunday. In Bilbao the Catholic churches are open. They are not open in Madrid because there has been no demand that they should be opened. The Basque representative in the Cabinet is a Catholic."

Of the battle of Guadalajara, the physician said it was not a defeat; it was a rout. The Garibaldi Battalion of Italian anti-Fascists were the happiest people in Spain on that day, he added.

"Before that battle," he said, "the Garibaldi Battalion had only one rifle to every three men. It had no shoes, no coats, no equipment. But the Fascists ran in such a hurry" ... and the physician chuckled as he recalled it ... "that after the battle the Loyalist battalions on that front were the best equipped in Spain. The Italians left everything, even their new camouflaged uniforms – the first we had ever seen. And in one stage of the rout, one Garibaldi battalion defeated an entire regular Italian regiment. It was the most amazing rout you could ever imagine.

Of Madrid itself, he said: "It is safer to live in Madrid than it is in New York or Montreal. There is no confusion. Everything is orderly. The jewellery shops are open. They display costly pieces in their windows. Life is normal except

128

Left behind on the Málaga–Almería road. (Hazen Sise. Library and Archives Canada PA-117427)

during a bombardment and then the people merely refuse to become panicky. Their spirit will not be broken."

In the grimness of the struggle, Dr. Bethune found some amusing angles.

"Do you know what we do with the Italian prisoners we capture? If they are wounded, we send them to hospital. I myself have given Fascists 15 blood transfusions. After they are better and they know that Madrid is not full of red hordes, we send them back to Italy. Sure we do. They'll make plenty of trouble for Mussolini. Plenty."

He showed your correspondent a banknote he had taken from a Moor. It was received by the black man as payment for fighting, a 1,000 mark note on the Reich bank dated April, 1910, worth less than the paper it was printed on.

"Yes," he repeated grimly, "with the proper arms, the Spanish people would beat Franco in a month easily. No matter what happens, they will never yield. But the democratic nations of the world may suffer for their sheer timidity in this so-called neutrality policy."

Touching briefly on the recent Deutschland incident and the German retaliation against the Spanish port of Almería, he described the shelling of the port as a "barbaric crime." The battleship Deutschland was in a place where it had no business to be, he said. The Spanish pilots who bombed her "and incidentally it was damn good bombing" said the warship fired on them first. "Probably it did," he said.

"But the retaliation against civilians was exactly the same as if the Spanish pilots, instead of striking a warship, had bombed a liner," he declared. Almería, he said, was a small port of no military importance. Ninety per cent of the victims were civilians.

Dr. Bethune said the morale of the Government-held portions of Spain was "higher now than ever before." In contrast, he affirmed "Franco is holding a deserted country." Dr. Bethune stated that 50 per cent of the civilian population of that part of Spain held by the insurgents had moved into the Government's territory. The reason, he said, was the fact that when insurgents entered a town they immediately shot all able-bodied men between 16 and 60, "unless they can prove they gave no aid to the enemy – an impossible thing to prove."

Dr. Bethune said he volunteered his services to the Canadian Red Cross to work in Spain, but the Red Cross advised him it was not sending units overseas.

The Canadian Committee for the Aid of Spanish Democracy then sent him over. Upon arrival at Madrid "we saw the need for a preserved blood service, so we started it."

He reached Madrid late in 1936 and got his unit in operation toward the end of the year.

*Montreal Gazette*, 8 June 1937

From New York, Bethune went to Toronto, where the CASD had arranged a hero's welcome for him. The following is a description of the rally held in his honour on June 14.

Warning his listeners not to be deceived that a world war would break out in six months or a year, Dr. Norman Bethune, [the] Montreal doctor who has returned after months of service to the Spanish loyalists, declared to a Queen's Park meeting last night that "the world war is on now. This battle –

A pensive Bethune after his return to Canada. (Photographer unknown. Library and Archives Canada PA-116900)

this world war," Dr. Bethune asserted, "will mean the end of fascism in the world today."

The doctor, with the iron gray hair and the soft, conversational voice, was given a thundering ovation at the intersection of York and Fleet Sts. About eight o'clock last night. He arrived in Toronto by automobile from Buffalo. Toronto radicals, headed by Communist leaders, massed at the intersection with many anti-fascist placards.

Two bands also greeted the Canadian doctor who organized and supervised the blood transfusion unit in Loyalist Spain. Dr. Bethune transferred from a closed to an open automobile and, accompanied by Rev. Ben Spence of the Canadian committee to aid Spanish loyalists, led a parade to Queen's Park. About 2,500 people gathered around the bandstand.

When Dr. Bethune stepped to the microphone three cheers roared from the throats of the gathering, most of whom emphasized the cheers with up thrust fists.

"Friends and comrades," the doctor opened. "Salutations from the anti-fascists of Spain to the anti-fascists of Canada. Salute!" Dr. Bethune's fist went up in the anti-fascist salute. "Fascism," he declared, "Is being defeated in Spain. There is a common united front of all peoples in Loyalist Spain. A same common, united front must be built up in Canada. No single party in Canada can defeat the common enemy that is on our doorstep. We must unite.

"If there is any lesson I have learned in Spain it is that the common front will defeat fascism. So far as Bilbao is concerned, things are bad. But Bilbao is not all of Spain. Bilbao may fall, but democracy in Spain will still conquer. The people of Spain are a grand people," the doctor declared. "Their fight is the fight of the workers of the world – the fight against fascism which is the world war that is on now."

Following his address one of a dozen girls dressed as Red Cross nurses presented him with a bouquet. Dr. Bethune, after thanking her, leaned over and kissed her. Immediately the other 11 were clamoring for similar treatment. Dr. Bethune complied, and went gallantly down the line of pretty girls.

Referring to the two victories of fascism, Japan's conquest of Manchuria and Italy's conquest of Ethiopia, Dr. Bethune declared the third great battle is being fought in Spain. "Be on guard against fascism in Canada and America," he warned.

"This work of mine is made possible by you people and could not go on without your aid, and hundreds of wounded men thank you," he said. "The workers are the backbone of this movement, and the white collar workers must realize their place is in this movement and join too," he said, amid applause.

"The Spanish loyalists must and will win," Dr. Bethune said, declaring that conditions for the Loyalists were not as bad as the capitalist press indicates.

*Toronto Daily Star*, 15 June 1937

The next day, William Strange, a freelance reporter, approached Bethune as he entered his hotel and asked for an interview. Bethune responded that he was between meetings, but if Strange were willing to conduct the interview while Bethune was taking a bath, he was free to accompany him to his room. Strange later wrote the following:

I talked yesterday for at least a full hour to a man whose name ought to figure in history some day. Not for what he may do in the future, either; but for what he has already done. He is a Canadian doctor, not a simple country doctor this time, but a scientific research man who has "gone practical" because he couldn't stand by and watch people dying like flies under the wheels of the Fascist juggernaut.

He is Dr. Norman Bethune of Montreal, back from Spain – "thoroughly fit but a bit tired," he told me – and boiling over with an implacable anger at things he has seen. I'm going to put the last question I asked him first, because it seems to me to give a key to the strong selfless character of this amazing man.

Bethune with soldiers in Madrid. (Attributed to Hazen Sise. Roderick Stewart collection)

"What induced you to go?" I asked him. "You must have known it was going to be no picnic. What drove you into the shambles?"

"Oh well, I guess I felt pretty sympathetic for the people," he said. "They were broadcasting appeals for help, and especially for doctors and medical supplies. And I ... well, I felt they weren't getting a break."

"So you went?"

"Yes, I went."

Simple, isn't it? The doctor just went. He resigned his jobs (note the plural) and departed on one of the most humane and noble expeditions ever undertaken by a member of a humane and noble profession. A measure of the work he has done may be taken from the fact that he has given 700 blood transfusions in Spain since January the first. And he's going back to give some more. "Oh yes, I'll go back." He tossed that assurance over his shoulder as he was shaving.

He has a very definite perspective on the horror that is modern Spain; and he wants to warn as many people as possible ... the whole world, I should think.

"What hardly anybody seems to realize," he said, "is that the world war has started already. It started even before the trouble broke out in Spain. It began in 1931 in Manchuria. The Fascists won that time. Then it got going again in Abyssinia, and the Fascists won again. Now it's coming out more clearly into the open. It ought to be plain to democratic countries what we're up against now, for the conflict is a straight fight between fascism and democracy."

"And will fascism win again in Spain, do you think?"

"Not a chance!" was the emphatic reply. "A famous Spanish writer made that plain enough to Franco just before he faced the firing squad. 'You may conquer us,' he told the Fascist leader, 'but you cannot win.'"

"And will they conquer?"

"I don't think so. I don't see how they can, for all the people that matter in Spain are against the Fascists."

"Will you clarify that a bit?" I requested. "Exactly whom do you mean by the people that matter?"

"Why, the workers, of course. The real people." He might have said "the simple people," for they are all the people that matter to him.

I thought at this point of a picture I had seen of Dr. Bethune taken on his arrival in Toronto and showing him saluting a cheering crowd with the famous clenched fist salute. "By the way, doctor, are you a Communist?" The question startled him.

"Most emphatically I am not," he said, "let's get this thing straight. You can call me a Socialist if you like. I am a Socialist in the same way that millions of sane people are Socialists. I want to see people getting a square deal, and I hate Fascism. The clenched fist is used as a 'People's Front' salute. It's used in Spain by everybody who is against the Fascists. That's really all it means – anti-Fascism. Why, Premier Blum of France uses it, and he's no Communist. I should describe it as a reply to the raised hand salute of the Fascist."

So we got that straight; and I'm glad we did, for no reader of this story will now be able to point at this quietly great humanitarian and make pretence that he's some kind of ogre in disguise.

"Now here's something I particularly want to ask'" I said. "How about the civilian population on the rebel side?"

"There aren't so very many," he replied grimly. "Franco is ruling over what is not very far from a deserted territory. There isn't much civilian population in his hands. The people knew what fascism would mean for them, so they got out. This accounts for a good deal of the congestion in the loyalist territory."

"That sounds like tragedy," I said.

"You're right there. It is tragedy, God knows."

"Do you know what those devils did?" he asked me. "They shot every trade-unionist they could lay hands on. They shot every man who had ever been on strike. They shot every mild Socialist. They shot school teachers who had at any time spoken favourably of democracy. Then after a while they went further than that. They rounded up everyone they could find who had worked for the democratic government of Spain – the legally elected government of their own country! And if these people could not prove positively that they had worked unwillingly for that government ... well, they shot them, too. This applied to every man from the ages of 16 to 60. My God, Mr. Strange, they've killed them by the hundred thousand!"

The doctor showed me a most impressive piece of paper money. It was handsomely printed and even fairly clean. It had been taken from a Moorish prisoner and I gathered that it represented a substantial proportion of his latest "pay-cheque." Here is what I read on it. "Reichsbanknote, 1,000 marks, Berlin, den 21 April, 1910." The doctor told me that Franco promises his mercenaries that this "money" will be redeemed after the war! Redeemed in what? one wonders. The 1,000-mark bill is worth less than the paper it is written on. When the Moors find out this swindle, may this redemption not be one of blood?

We discussed Bilbao. "Yes," said Dr. Bethune gravely, "the news from there is bad, real bad. But this is something that I want to make a particular point of. It hasn't fallen yet ... and it may not fall at all. Those Roman Catholic Basques will fight to the last man, and the street-fighting is going to be a bitter struggle. So bitter that I have no hesitation in saying that [nationalist commander] Davila's real struggle has only just begun. By the way," he broke off for a moment, "I do wish you'd stress that Roman Catholic business. These people are genuine Catholics, and they won't give up their religion whatever happens. They haven't been excommunicated, and it's hopelessly wrong for people to think that it is not possible to be anti-fascist and Roman Catholic at one and the same time."

I asked what the Spanish thought of Britain's attitude. "They are completely bewildered," he told me. "They have always trusted in Britain and looked upon her as the world's great democratic bulwark. They're not angry but they are terribly puzzled and a good deal hurt. They are like children whose father is letting them take a licking without lifting a finger to help. They simply cannot understand it."

"And what is your own opinion of the British attitude?" Dr. Norman Bethune is what might well be described as a forceful humanitarian. At this point he got forceful. "Cynical" and "hypocritical" were two of his adjectives: but they were not the strongest. "My own theory about the British attitude is a very simple one. England is an imperialist, capitalist country possessed of enormous vested interests in various parts of the world, and these are loosely held together by a cement of sentimentality. She is determined to have a weak Spain in order to keep clear her trade route to India. Twenty per cent of Britain's oil supply comes down the Iraq pipe lines and through the Mediterranean; 25 per cent of her raw material imports pass through the Mediterranean. And Mussolini is determined to make the Mediterranean an Italian lake.

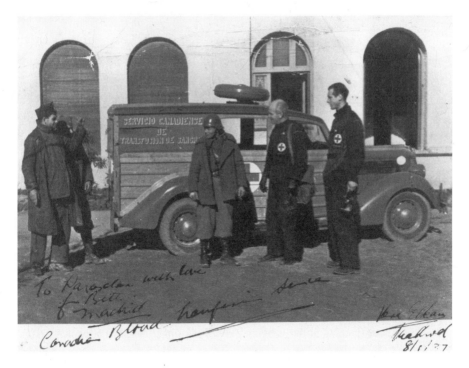

Bethune and Sise in front of the Instituto canadiense. (Photographer unknown. Library and Archives Canada PA-116904)

"If this were to happen Britain would lose control of Iraq, Egypt and India. Now what we believe is this: That Britain knows a clash with Italy is inevitable, unless Italy goes bankrupt. The British government is playing a deep game. It is willing to let Spain fight Britain's battle in the Mediterranean. Britain has nothing to fear even from a Communist Spain, but she will never allow a Fascist victory. If the Fascists came really close to victory, Britain and France would intervene at once. Otherwise the war can go on, hundreds and thousands of men and women may die and the British will do nothing as long as their commercial interests are not threatened."

This was strong meat. "You're sure that's for publication?" He answered the question with another: "Do you think we could let this go on without getting up and shouting about it?" So I asked him next if he thought there was any chance of Great Britain, Canada and the United States coming together in an effort to preserve peace and to bring about the betterment of the world.

"Whatever our ideals may be there is no hope for peace until people realize that the causes of war are economic," he replied. "Under the present rule of hopeless economic chaos I don't see any chance of eliminating war. It's a matter of international justice much more than one of policemen."

And there are Canadians there. Dr. Bethune knows many of them – "wonderful boys" he called them. There are 500 or so, on the Loyalist side. "And the rebel side?" "I don't know of any," the doctor said. "None that I've heard of." I think it would hurt him if there were.

"Any Canadian girls there, too?" "Quite a few nurses," he said. And he had a word or two to say of Toronto's "Jimmy" (Jean) Watts. She does a weekly newscast from Madrid. Did he know her? Well, he ought to. "She lives in our own institution," he explained with a chuckle.

And a word about that institution. "Yes, you can call it a great success, at least from the experimental point of view. We've drawn and used 90 gallons of blood for transfusions this year and now it's been taken over by the Spanish military doctors, and it is being extended right through the loyalist organization. And don't say we 'can' blood. We are able to preserve it now and use it days after it has been drawn from the donor; but it isn't 'canned'!"

Then came something that had a particular meaning. "I hate fascism." Those words came early in this amazing tale of a doctor who risked his life (and is going to risk it again) to bring succour to his suffering fellow men. "I hate fascism."

*Toronto Daily Star*, 16 June 1937

Bethune arrived in Montreal two days later and spoke at a large rally of enthusiastic supporters of Republican Spain. Bethune and leading CASD members took special delight at the success of the meeting, not only because the overflow crowd donated nearly $2000 for the blood transfusion unit, but because it was held in the Mount Royal Arena, the very place where the planned CASD meeting of nine months earlier had been blocked by the city council.

Two weeks later he began a speaking tour that would take him across Canada to the Pacific and Atlantic coasts and into the United States, where he spoke in several large cities. The schedule was tight. Between early July and mid-September he spoke almost daily, making two and often three speeches at every stop along his route. In his addresses, which he quickly learned to deliver with considerable skill, he described the horrors of the war. Initially, his appeal for funds was directed toward maintaining the work of the Instituto, but he spoke with increasing frequency of his Children's City project, which he had finally persuaded the CASD to adopt. Eventually, with money raised by Bethune and sent to Spain by the CASD, two refuges for children were built in Catalonia. The rest of the donations made by people who were moved by his oratory was used to maintain support for the Madrid transfusion unit.

The CASD hoped that a broad cross-section of the Canadian populace, very few of whom were sympathetic to Communist ideas, would attend rallies at which Bethune was the featured speaker. Realizing that knowledge of his political affiliation could deflect many potential donors, at the outset of the tour Communist leaders instructed Bethune to conceal his Party membership. During the first few weeks of the tour, as William Strange had done in his interview with Bethune, many people posed the same question: "Are you a Communist?" Bethune, who believed that it was natural and desirable to reveal one's deeply held beliefs, managed with the greatest difficulty to adhere to Party strictures until the night of July 20 in Winnipeg, Manitoba. The following is an account of that evening:

"I have the honor to be a Communist," said Dr. Norman Bethune, to whom nearly a hundred friends gave a banquet at the St. Charles hotel, Tuesday night. Describing his conversion, he told how, two years ago, he had visited London, Eng., and seen "women and children starving in the slums," and then had gone to Moscow and found there the healthiest women and children he had ever seen.

"I didn't care then," he continued, "what the system was called, but I knew that what we wanted was the thing those Russians had got. The Russian women were not so sex-conscious as western women. They looked one straight in the face and walked like queens.

"I am reminded of the time when Alice asked if she could be a queen and the white Queen answered her: 'Yes, my dear, you'll be a queen, but you'll start as a pawn and when we get to the ninth square we'll all be queens together.' That is the idea of communism – we'll start as pawns and in the end, we'll all be kings and queens together."

"The exploitation of women by men, which has gone on too long in other countries," he declared, "has been ended in Russia. That is why every woman,

Sise taking photographs.
(Photographer unknown.
Library and Archives Canada
PA-172311)

unless she is just a bundle of sensuous nerve-endings, must be either a
Socialist or a Communist. You women could stop war – just as the clergymen
of the last generation could have stopped the Great War, if they had had the
courage to say it was against the will of Christ. Why don't you women unite
and give up this sense of property?"

"The men who are fighting in the government forces in Spain are fighting
for you just as much as did the men in the Great War. It is a better thing to
fight for democracy than to fight for your king and country. Canada's time
of agony has not come yet, but it will come. Do not despair if the bourgeois
class will no co-operate with you. When the clash comes they will melt like
snow. We bourgeois must humble ourselves before the workers, not go down
to them but go up to them and ask them if we may help them in their work."

Among sidelights on the Spanish war given by Dr. Bethune were the facts
that the Canadians in the international brigade stayed in the trenches for 90
days on end – a longer period than any brigade had known during the World
War; that Russian pilots never refused battle but flew straight into an enemy
machine, regardless of the almost certain death that failure would bring;
that during the past winter the greatest need among the international
brigade was for cigarettes. "The government forces will never be conquered,"
he ended, "because they know what they are fighting for and the Fascists do
not. That was why 500 government Italians without boots put to flight a
highly-mechanized brigade of 5,000 Italians on the Fascist side. The women

in Madrid stand in queues a quarter of a mile long to get a handful of beans. They have no meat but they tell their men to go on fighting. You cannot defeat people like that," concluded Dr. Bethune.

*Winnipeg Free Press*, 22 July 1937

Having vented his deep desire to cry out his beliefs, Bethune felt only temporary relief. He was still not happy playing the role of propagandist. He had accepted it as a form of penance for his errant behaviour in Spain. "I have blotted my copybook," he had admitted to Sise. But as soon as he could, he wanted to go back to Spain. Two days after admitting publicly that he was a Communist, he cabled Sise, Sorensen, and May in Madrid to inform them that at the end of the tour he intended to go back to Spain to join the International Brigades. Sise immediately notified both the Spanish and Canadian Communist parties of Bethune's proposed action.

Two weeks later Bethune was in British Columbia, where he began to show the film *Heart of Spain*, which had been sent to him days after its completion in New York. The following is a newspaper account of a meeting where the film had its first showing.

Despite perfect midsummer weather which sent thousands of people flocking to parks and beaches in vacation mood, progressive Vancouver citizens packed the Orpheum theatre to the last seat in the gallery on Sunday to hear Dr. Norman Bethune, noted Canadian surgeon whose work as director of the Spanish-Canadian Blood Transfusion Institute in Spain has brought him world recognition, and to see 'The Heart of Spain', "first authentic cinematic record of the Spanish war to be shown here."

Long before the hour scheduled for the meeting the crowds began to gather and hundreds of late-comers without tickets were turned away.

If the stark realism – glimpses of children's bodies being lifted from shattered houses, of troops of the People's Army on the offensive, of the actual work of the Canadian medical unit and, throughout it all, a woman's heartrending sobs – were not enough to rouse a sympathetic audience, then Dr. Bethune himself with his human approach to the many questions he touched upon, his free style interspersed with ready humor, brought his audience out of its seats in a spontaneous demonstration worthy of a people's front.

Worsley (left) and Bethune with refugees in Almería.
(Hazen Sise. Roderick Stewart collection)

Dr. Bethune stepped to the microphone, raising his hand in the clenched fist salute of the people's front. As one man, the audience rose cheering to return the salute.

"This is our answer to the challenge of Fascism – the anti-Fascist salute," he declared. "It isn't the property of the Communists, the Socialists or the Republicans. It's the salute of all anti-Fascists."

From the scathing denunciation of the capitalist press for its distortion of news in Spain, in which he asserted that many of the correspondents in Madrid disclaimed reports as published as not truthful reproductions of the news they had sent; Dr. Bethune passed on to speak of socialized medicine.

"I have been advocating it for years," he said. "I don't know that a five-dollar bill should be allowed to stand between a man and his doctor. Medicine should be free and supported by taxation.

"Naturally, the greatest part of the burden should be borne by the wealthy to whose interest it is that the working man whom they exploit and from whose labor they derive their wealth should be healthy."

Sorensen, Carmen (a Spanish nurse), Sise, Celia Greenspan, and Bethune shortly
after the opening of the Instituto canadiense. (Photographer unknown.
Roderick Stewart collection)

From socialized medicine, Dr. Bethune went on to tell of the development
of the Canadian medical unit with a single ambulance to "the present
Spanish-Canadian Blood Transfusion Institute carrying on its vital work on
every front."

The Institute now has five cars and a staff of 25, including doctors, technicians, nurses and chauffeurs.

"It's really a glorified milk service," he said with a quick smile, "only, instead of milk it's blood, the safe delivery of which means all the difference
between life and death."

Dr. Bethune stated that the work of the Canadian medical unit and the
heroism of the Mackenzie-Papineau battalion, composed of Canadian anti-
Fascist volunteers, provided an issue, perhaps the first, on which all progressive people could unite to save democracy, the front line of which lay in the
trenches of Spain.

"I have seen the practical advantages of the people's front in action in
Spain," he declared. "Without the strength of unity no single party could

143

have withstood the onslaught of Fascism. And therefore, because I see in Canada the first signs of Fascism, I realize how urgent is the need for building a people's front in this country.

"A people's front is necessary here unless we wish to have such horrors as you have seen on the screen tonight visited upon us."

Relating some of his experiences in Spain, Dr. Bethune stated that hundreds of blood transfusions had been given to Italian prisoners whose fear that they would be shot had changed to amazement at the kindness with which they were treated.

"When they are well we send them back to Italy," he said. "They're the finest anti-Fascist propaganda in the world."

The Spanish-Canadian Blood Transfusion Institute has set up a second institute in Valencia, Dr. Bethune stated, and is planning to set up a third on the Cordoba front.

He appealed particularly for the Spanish children. Of 500,000 children in Spain, 100,000 are orphans, he said. "We want to set up a 'Little Canada' in Spain, removed from the scenes of War, where these children will be sate from German and Italian planes.

"There will be a Toronto, a Winnipeg, a Vancouver block. We want Canadian organizations to adopt children. Pictures will be sent and organizations will be able to pick the children they wish to adopt. After the war they can visit here. It will be á new link of international brotherhood."

*The People's Advocate* [Vancouver], 6 August 1937

Shortly after his appearance in Vancouver, Bethune learned that his plan to return to Spain had been turned down. That pill may have been even more bitter than the one that he had swallowed on leaving there three months earlier. His censure by both the Canadian Communist party and by Spanish authorities hurt him profoundly, for he felt it was a punishment far too harsh for his misdemeanors. And he was right. Bethune's acts of mercy toward civilians on the Málaga road, the daily performance of his Madrid unit in carrying blood to wounded Republican soldiers, and his concern for the welfare of children and determination to find the most humane solutions for the problem of the war orphans merit the highest praise. Already known in Canada for his

144

dedication to the most disadvantaged, in Spain Bethune became a doctor without borders who unselfishly worked – always as a doctor – to go to the aid of the defenceless.

But that was not all. Norman Bethune was also one of the most important propagandists for the Republican cause. When the Instituto canadiense de transfusión de sangre began to function in Madrid in December, 1936, he described the work of his unit in reports to Canada that became the source of inspiration for Canadians to donate thousands of dollars to help the Spanish people. His radio broadcasts also reached many listeners. His shocked reaction to the merciless treatment of helpless women and children fleeing toward Almería, which impelled him to write *The Crime on the Road*, drew international attention to this atrocity. *Heart of Spain*, the harrowing 30-minute documentary film that he made possible, was seen by tens of thousands of North Americans, inspiring sympathy for the Republic. And, finally, his gruelling North American speaking tour raised a substantial sum of money for Spain and increased public awareness of the struggle of the majority of its people against Fascism.

Many fighters in the International Brigades laid down their lives for the cause of the Republic. But, aside from those who made that ultimate sacrifice, no Canadian and arguably few other foreigners did so much for the benefit of Republican Spain as Norman Bethune. Surely the contradictions in his personality make him more human and the accomplishments he made despite them all the more admirable: with the perspective of time, the personal failings that led to his recall to Canada cannot but be eclipsed by his inestimable contributions to Republican Spain.

**10** ◆ O T H E R
H O R I Z O N S

Bethune's fears concerning the operation of the Instituto by the Sanidad Militar were soon realized. Although Canadian donations collected by the CASD and sent to Madrid continued until the end of the war, the Instituto hispano-canadiense de transfusión de sangre became more and more Spanish and less Canadian. By the late autumn of 1937, only months after Bethune's departure, Henning Sorensen and Hazen Sise had returned to Canada.

Despite his humiliation and anger at the rejection of his plan to return to Spain, Bethune soon turned his attention to a possible new path. He was keeping informed of rapidly escalating developments in China after the outbreak of hostilities between Japanese and Chinese forces in July 1937. This new interest coincided with his growing awareness that because of his publicly stated political beliefs it would not be easy for him to find employment. Not only Sacré-Coeur, but many non-Catholic hospitals as well would not be willing to offer a position to an avowed Communist Party member. Alone in his personal life, without an income, uncertain of his professional future, and still smarting from his disturbing Spanish experience, he started to look into the possibility of going to China to play some role in the struggle against the imperialist forces of Japan.

After his last fundraising speech in Montreal in October, Bethune went to New York at the invitation of the China Aid Council, a recently formed group that planned to aid China in its struggle against Japan. They agreed to send Dr. Charles Parsons, an American surgeon, Jean Ewen, a Canadian nurse, and Bethune as a medical unit to China. On 8 January 1938, they left Vancouver for Hong Kong aboard the *Empress of Asia*. This was the beginning of the last and most significant phase of Bethune's life. Soon after reaching China, the unit broke up and Bethune found his way in June to a remote mountainous region southwest of Beijing where he was appointed medical advisor to the Chinese Communist Eighth Route Army, which was engaged in guerilla warfare with a highly trained and superbly equipped Japanese army.

For the next seventeen months, Bethune's activities made him far more than a medical advisor. His initial plan was to inspect and revamp the existing Eighth Route Army health facilities, which were located throughout an area larger than half of Spain's. As the only Western-trained surgeon in the army, he was also needed to tend to wounded Chinese soldiers. To perform this role, he led a mobile medical-surgical unit that, when summoned by military commanders, travelled by horseback to positions near the fighting. There, in improvised operating theatres frequently under enemy fire, Bethune and his team treated the wounded in battles that sometimes lasted for several days.

In the brief periods between campaigns, he devised medical instruments and other devices suitable for use in dealing with casualties of guerilla warfare. In an attempt to create an army medical service equipped with rudimentary medical and surgical skills, he set up brief training sessions for which he gave lectures and wrote textbooks. The situation was dramatically different from that of Spain, where he had played an outstanding role among a group of crusaders who had come to fight Fascism. Now, lost in the immensity of China, immersed in a foreign culture, completely isolated from the external world, and utterly dedicated to his work as a doctor, Bethune at last attained a measure of personal contentment and respect. He wrote, "It is true I am tired, but I don't think I have been so happy for a long time. I am content. I am doing what I want to do. Why shouldn't I be happy ... I am needed."

Despite the satisfaction of his extraordinary achievements and of working with people he admired in their struggle against the Japanese invader, he was running himself into the ground. Constantly on the move, eating poorly, and seldom having an opportunity to rest, he was visibly in failing heath by the summer of 1939. Photographs taken at the time show a frail and gaunt white-haired man who appeared to be in his late sixties. Norman Bethune was only forty-nine.

In mid-August, he set up a medical school and a small training hospital. Realizing that he must have foreign financial support for it, he decided to return to North America for a brief fundraising tour. On the eve of his planned departure in October, he cut the middle finger of his left hand while operating on a wounded soldier. The finger became infected and blood poisoning soon developed. In his weakened condition and without proper medicine, he became mortally ill. Two weeks later, on November 12, in a one-room peasant house, surrounded by the helpless, tearful members of his team, Bethune died.

Near the end of December 1939, Mao Zedong wrote a short essay, "In Memory of Norman Bethune," in which he praised the selfless spirit of this foreigner who not only made the long trip to China to help it in its hour of peril, but gave his life for the cause. Nearly thirty years later, at the height of the Great Proletarian Cultural Revolution, Mao's essay became one of his three most-read articles, which were designed to inspire the Chinese people to rededicate themselves to the aims of Mao's ideal of Communism. Millions of people dutifully committed the essay to memory.

Because of Mao's essay, Bethune became a Chinese hero during the late 1960s. The hospital he had set up in the barren region where he died was transferred to the large rail-junction city of Shijiazhuang. Given the name Bethune International Peace Hospital, it is today a modern 800-bed institution. Adjacent to it is the Norman Bethune Military Medical College, and a short distance away, in a memorial park dedicated to the martyrs in the war against Japan and the subsequent civil war with the Nationalists, lie Bethune's remains. His tomb and a nearby museum dedicated to his life and career constitute the focal point of the park.

In the land of his birth there was no similar recognition. Other than to family members and the small number of Canadian Communists, his name remained virtually unknown until the early 1970s, when Canada and China established diplomatic relations. Upon his return from a state visit to China in 1973, Prime Minister Pierre Trudeau made arrangements for the purchase of the house in which Bethune was born in the town of Gravenhurst. Trudeau's action, prompted by the frequent requests of Chinese delegations to Canada to visit the house, was taken in the interest of Sino-Canadian relations and of getting a Canadian entree into the huge Chinese economic market. Restored to period, the building was opened as the Bethune Memorial House in 1976. The majority of its visitors continue to be Chinese – tourists from China, members of business or government delegations, and a steadily growing number of Chinese Canadians.

In Spain, too, Bethune was little known, as indeed was the tragic flight of the Málaga refugees in which he and his two companions performed so nobly. Until recently it had been widely believed that the attack by German and Italian airplanes on the defenceless town of Guernica in northern Spain on 26 April 1937, which resulted in several hundred deaths, was the most heinous atrocity of the Spanish Civil War. Because the Nationalists came out of the war as victors, and their leader, Francisco Franco, held power until his death in 1975, no attempt was made during those years to determine the number of people who had been massacred by Nationalist and Italian forces on the road to Almería during that second week of February 1937. Although it will always remain impossible to document the extent of the loss of life, it is now generally believed that the Málaga to Almería flight greatly surpassed Guernica in its horror.

This conclusion, resulting from research in the 1990s, also inspired an increased interest in Bethune and led, in 1996, to the Spanish Association of Canadian Studies' publication of *Homenaje a Norman Bethune* (*Homage to Norman Bethune*). During the next few years, Jésus Majada found and interviewed survivors of the exodus from Málaga to Almería and also collected photographs, many of them taken by Hazen Sise during their flight. Combining these with explanatory texts comprising excerpts from his interviews and passages from Bethune's *The Crime on the Road: Málaga–Almería*, he created a photographic exhibition that revealed the enormity of the atrocity. Entitled *Norman Bethune: el crimen de la carretera de Málaga–Almería*, the exhibition was displayed in Málaga in 2004 with the financial assistance of the Centro Andaluz de Fotografía.

Bethune portrait taken in Paris in February 1937. (Photographer unknown. Library and Archives Canada PA-195385)

This was followed less than two years later by an event held on 7 February 2006, when the city of Málaga paid a long-overdue debt. In a ceremony attended by Marc Lortie, the Canadian ambassador, a maple tree was planted and a bronze plaque with the heading *Paseo de los canadienses* (Promenade of the Canadians) was raised at a pretty spot along the city waterfront where, sixty-nine years before, the fugitives had passed as they streamed out of the city. Below the heading was written, "In memory of the help given by the people of Canada through the actions of Norman Bethune to fleeing Malagueñans in 1937."

After Málaga, Jesús Majada's exhibition was shown in a dozen Spanish cities before being sent to Canada. To mark the seventieth anniversary of Bethune's death, *Norman Bethune: The Trail of Solidarity*, an expanded version of *Norman Bethune: el crimen de la carretera de Málaga–Almería*, was on display at the McCord Museum in Montreal throughout 2009, a year declared by civic authorities as one of "homage to Norman Bethune."

Days before his departure for Spain in 1936, Bethune wrote, "Born a bourgeois; died a Communist." Largely because of his political faith, and despite various forms of recognition of his achievements, including biographies, stage plays, and films, many Canadians and some Spaniards have been reluctant to consider him a hero. But the figure of Norman Bethune transcends ideology and goes beyond standard political definitions. His humanitarianism, his concern for the disadvantaged, his indifference to material interests, his dedication to defending a principle, and his conviction that each individual is capable of changing the world offer inspiration to those who fight for justice.

Perhaps, as the embers of the Cold War die out, new generations will be inclined to judge the man less for his political ideas and more by the testimony of his life's achievements.

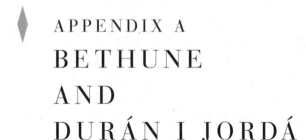

APPENDIX A

# BETHUNE AND DURÁN I JORDÁ

The relationship between Norman Bethune and Frederic Durán i Jordà has been a matter of some controversy. In Spain some believe that, shortly after his arrival from Canada in 1936, Bethune visited Durán i Jordà and took from him the idea of putting into operation a blood transfusion service. On this question, see the following:

• Carol Archs, José. *Federico Durán-Jordá, el combatiente de la sangre*. Barcelona: Ediciones Rondas, 1978.

• Grífols i Espés, Joan. *Frederic Duran i Jordà: un métode, una época*. Barcelona: Hemo-Institut Grifols, 1997.

• Carballo, Navarro and José Ramón. *Frederic Duran i Jordà: un hito en la historia de la transfusión sanguínea*. Madrid: Ministerio de Defensa, Secretaría General Técnica, 2005.

• Massons, Josep M. "L'obra de Frederic Duran i Jordà viscuda per mi." *Revista de la Reial Acadèmia de Medicina de Catalunya* 21, no. 2 (2006): 52–55.

• Monferrer Catalán, Luis. *Odisea en Albión: Los republicanos españoles exiliados en Gran Bretaña*. Madrid: Ediciones de la Torre, 2007. p. 233.

• Lozano Molero, Miguel, and Joan Cid. "Frederic Duran-Jorda: a transfusion medicine pioneer." *Transfusion Medicine Reviews*. 21, no. 1 (2007): 75–81.

Dr. Moises Broggi (1908–2012), an eminent surgeon who during the war worked in trucks converted into operating theatres and field hospitals, indicated in correspondence with Roderick Stewart (10 July 2003) that he had met Bethune in the Hotel Florida in May 1937. He wrote: "I remember that when I told him that I came from Barcelona, he showed much interest in the work and the transfusion service of Duran i Jordà whom he visited when he passed through our city in November 1936." It is precisely the idea initiated by Broggi's statement that has generated the thesis that Bethune's procedure was derived from that of Durán i Jordà.

We believe, however, that this is not correct. Norman Bethune visited Durán i Jordà on two occasions. On the first occasion, in February 1937, he was introduced to Durán i Jordà's system and examined the vehicles he used; as a result, accompanied by Sorensen, he went to Marseille, where he bought the Renault. Returning to Barcelona a week later, he discussed with the Spanish doctor changes to the Renault that would need to be made to give to it the features of Durán i Jordà's vehicles.

It is true that Bethune had been in Barcelona at the beginning of December 1936 on returning from his trip to England and France. Together with Sorensen and Sise he had to spend a night in the city because the Ford had broken down. We do not believe that Bethune knew about Durán i Jordà at that time. Otherwise, he would have used the Durán i Jordà's techniques, which were superior to his own. In addition, in interviews with Roderick Stewart, neither Sorensen nor Sise mentioned that Bethune had met Durán i Jordà on that occasion in December.

It is more than likely that Bethune learned of Durán i Jordà after he had taken over the apartment on Príncipe de Vergara. In summary:

• Bethune's transfusion procedure was different from that of Durán i Jordà.

• Bethune conceived of the idea of a blood transfusion service without knowing of the existence of Durán i Jordà's method.

• Durán i Jordà had already developed his technology some months before Bethune started his service.

• Durán i Jordà's method was superior to that of Bethune, a fact recognized by Bethune.

Although Bethune had performed blood transfusions in Montreal, and took some blood transfusion equipment with him to Spain, he did not leave Canada with the preconceived purpose of establishing a blood transfusion service in Spain.

# APPENDIX B
# FOREIGN
# MEMBERS
# OF THE
# INSTITUTO

HAZEN SISE (1906–1974) was born into a prominent Montreal family. Graduating in architecture from the Massachusetts Institute of Technology in 1929, to continue his studies and to find employment he went to France, and then England, where he met Bethune in 1936. From Spain in 1937 he returned to Canada. A staff member of the National Film Board of Canada during the Second World War, he later returned to the practice of architecture. Highly respected in Montreal art circles, he was also a gifted photographer. Those skills allowed him to record on film many poignant scenes during the flight from Málaga to Almería. The true historical significance of those photographs has come to light only in the past few years with the recognition of the significance of the Málaga–Almería atrocity. Because the collection of those photographs is the only known graphic record of that tragedy, it is considered in Spain to be an invaluable contribution to the Recovery of the Historical Memory, a project begun in 2006 to encourage research into atrocities committed during the Spanish Civil War.

HENNING SORENSEN (1901–1986), a Danish-Canadian, left his position as a translator in Montreal in September 1936 to go to Spain. After meeting Bethune in Madrid, he gave up his plan to report to a Copenhagen newspaper on the war and became Bethune's interpreter. During World War Two he served in the Royal Canadian Navy; later, he worked for the Canadian Broadcasting Corporation. After a brief period in Cuba in the 1960s as a translator, he returned to Canada, eventually retiring in North Vancouver, British Columbia.

ALLEN MAY (1907?–1945?), born in Elfros, Saskatchewan, was a journalist who wrote at various times *for Maclean's, Liberty*, and the *Globe and Mail*. The last Canadian to leave the Instituto, he apparently ended his life by suicide.

JEAN WATTS (1910–1968) graduated with a BA from the University of Toronto. A reporter with the *Daily Clarion* of Toronto, she assisted operations in the Instituto from February 1937 until her return to Canada later that summer. During the Second World War she served in the Canadian Women's Army Corps. In the 1960s she became active in an organization called The Voice of Women.

GEZA KÁRPÁTHI (1907–1998), a Hungarian who became a skilled photographer, travelled to the United States with Bethune in 1937 and subsequently had a successful career there in television and movies, using the screen name Charles Korvin.

HERMANN J. MULLER (1890–1967), an American geneticist, spent several weeks in early 1937 working with Bethune and J.B.S. Haldane on the use of cadaver blood. He later won a Nobel Prize in Physiology in 1946.

J.B.S. HALDANE (1892–1964), a renowned British geneticist, visited the Institute briefly in December 1936 and stayed there for a period of weeks early in 1937.

VERA ELKAN (1908–2008), a South African living in London, arrived in Madrid in December 1936 to make a film on the International Brigades. When Haldane introduced her to Bethune, he offered her a room in the Instituto. During her month-long stay she filmed Bethune and other members of the blood unit in action, in addition to photographing events in and around Madrid.

THOMAS WORSLEY (1907–1977), an Englishman, went to Spain in 1937 with Stephen Spender. He later became an author and theatre and television critic in England. His *roman à clef, Behind the Battle* (1939), provides a valuable source of information about Bethune during the two months he spent in the Instituto.

CELIA GREENSPAN (1907–2005), an American laboratory technician, set up and managed the laboratory at the Instituto until the end of January 1937, when she left to work in other areas. She returned to New York in November.

# BIBLIOGRAPHY

Associación Española de Estudios Canadienses. *Homenaje a Norman Bethune: Cuaderno conmemorativo del LX aniversario de su llegada en España*. Laguna: Universidad de Laguna, 1996.

Allan, Ted, and Sydney Gordon. *The Scalpel, the Sword: The Story of Doctor Norman Bethune*. With an introduction by Julie Allan, Dr. Norman Allan and Susan Ostrovsky. Toronto: Dundurn Press, 2009.

Bethune, Norman. *The Crime on the Road Málaga-Almería: narrative with graphic documents revealing fascist cruelty*. Pamphlet. Madrid: Publicaciones Iberia, 1937.

Bethune, Norman. *El Crimen de la carretera Málaga-Almería*. Translated by Jesús Majada Neila. Benalmádena Málaga: Caligrama, 2004.

Hannant, Larry. *The Politics of Passion: Norman Bethune's Writing and Art*. Toronto: University of Toronto Press, 1998

Majada Neila, Jesus, and Fernando Bueno Pérez. *Carretera Málaga-Almería (February 1937.)* Benalmádena Málaga: Caligrama, 2006.

Majada Neila, Jesús. *La Huella Solidaria – Trail of Solidarity – La Trace Solidaire* – Almería: Centro Andaluz de la Fotografia, 2008.

Shepherd, David A. E., and Andrée Lévesque, eds. Norman Bethune: His times and his legacy. Ottawa: Canadian Public Health Association, 1982

Stewart, Roderick. *Bethune.* Montréal: Editions du Jour, 1976.

Stewart, Roderick. *The Mind of Norman Bethune.* Markham, Ont.: Fitzhenry & Whiteside, 2002.

Worsley, Thomas C. *Behind the Battle.* London: Robert Hale Limited, 1939

# FILMOGRAPHY

*Heart of Spain.* 30 min. Directed by Herbert Kline and Geza Kárpáthi. Cinematography by Herbert Kline and Geza Kárpáthi. Frontier Films, 1937.

*Bethune: The Making of a Hero.* 115 min. Directed by Philip Borsos. Written by Ted Allan. Starring Donald Sutherland. Filmline International, 1990.

*Bethune.* 53 min. Directed by Donald Brittain. National Film Board of Canada, 1964.

# INDEX

Albacete, 21, 107

Alicante, 67, 68

Allan, Ted, 108, 111–12, 116

Almería: flight of refugees toward, 1, 65, 68, 70–5, 79–82, 145, 149; bombing of, 76–8, 83, 130

Araquistáin, Gertrude, 87

Araquistáin, Luis, 16

Archibald, Dr. Edward, 8, 9, 23

Barcelona, 26; base of Dr. Frederic Durán i Jordà's mobile blood transfusion unit, 23, 56, 153; centre of unified blood transfusion service, 57, 58, 60; Children's City project, 88, 90, 109

Bethune, Henry Norman: abuse of alcohol, 110–11, 112; accused of being a Fascist in Madrid, 18–19; admits he is a Communist, 139; aids downed French airmen, 75– 6; aids refugees on Málaga–Almería road, 70–4, 80–3; aids victims of bombing of Almería, 76–8; blood transfusion, knowledge of, 21–3, 29; character of, 4, 7–8, 110–11, 145; Children's City project, 87–92, 109, 123; deals with functioning of Instituto, 62, 101–9; family history of, 3–4; homecoming rallies for in Toronto and Montreal, 130–2; ignores orders of Sanidad Militar, 112–13; interest in art, 6, 9, 117–22; interest in Spanish Civil War, 12–13; joins Communist Party of Canada, 10; loses autonomous control of Instituto, 62, 93; medical training in London, 5–6; medical training in Montreal, 8; medical training in Toronto, 4–5; military service, 5–6; mission to

China, 146–8; mobile blood transfusion service in Spain, 21, 23–5, 27–31, 52–3, 58, 60, 95, 99, 130; newspaper articles about: 125–38, 139–44; offers services in Madrid hospitals, 20; offers services to International Brigades, 20; ordered to conceal his Communism, 10, 135, 139; personal problems in Spain, 110–12; political evolution, 9; propagandist for Republican cause, 145; proposes system of medicare in Canada, 10–11; public speaking, 11, 14, 138–45; refused permission to return to Spain, 144; rescues French airmen at Castell de Ferro, 75–6; resigns from Instituto, 115–16; returns from Spain to Canada, 123–4; suggests end to Canadian role in Instituto, 114; surgical training in Edinburgh, 6; unified blood transfusion service, 55–61, 63–4, 86, 93–4; visits front at battle of Guadalajara, 95–6; visits Republican hospitals in Guadarrama Mountains, 32, 35–6. *See also* Bethune's broadcasts, speeches and writings

Bethune, Frances Campbell Penney, 6, 7, 8

Bethune's broadcasts, speeches and writings: battle of Guadalajara, 95–6; bombing of Almería, 83–5; bombing of Madrid, 45–7, 52; care of sick and wounded in Madrid, 37–40; Children's City project, 88–92, 109, 123–4; Committee to Aid Spanish democracy, 32; functioning of the Instituto, 106–10; humanitarianism, 34–5; International Brigades, 42–3, 52, 95–100; loss of autonomy of Instituto, 114; Málaga–Almería road refugee disaster, 78–85; mobile blood transfusion service, 14–15, 24–5, 27–32, 52–3; poetry on the Spanish Civil War, 13–14, 48; radio broadcasts in Spain, 32–4, 37–40, 41–3, 44–7, 49–50; resignation from Instituto, 115–16; role of the artist as revolutionary, 117–22; significance of Spain's struggle against Fascism, 34, 40, 53–4; socialized medicine, 11; unified blood transfusion service, 58, 60, 63; wartime conditions in Madrid, 17, 31, 44–7; World War I contrasted with Spanish Civil War, 49–50

blood transfusions: Bethune's knowledge of, 21–3, 29, 52–3; methodology, 21–2, 29, 52–3, 58

Buck, Tim, 112

CASD. *See* Committee to Aid Spanish Democracy

Castell de Ferro, 75

Cerrada, Colonel: initial support for unified blood transfusion service, 56, 59; delays approval of

resignation to, 115; critical of Bethune's conduct, 113; rejects Bethune as leader of unified blood transfusion service, 93; reorganization of, 62, 113–14. *See also* Cerrada, Colonel

Sanz Vilaplana, Dr. Andrés, 101, 104, 110

Sarasola, Father Luis, 14, 15

Scott, Marian, 11

shortwave station EAQ (Madrid), 32–4, 37–40, 41–3, 44–7, 49–50

Sise, Hazen, 36, 126, 137, 146, 155; captain in Sanidad Militar, 62, 63; driver and organizer of transport for Instituto, 24, 31, 60, 63, 108, 116; helps prevent Bethune from returning to Spain, 141; in Barcelona, 57–8, 59, 60, 153; in Valencia, 63, 64; involved in Children's City project, 87–8, 92; Málaga–Almería road tragedy, 67, 70–6, 78, 83; meets Bethune in London and returns with him to Spain, 24; photographs of, 24, 35, 56, 59, 74, 93, 102, 123, 137, 140, 143; problems of/reorganization of Instituto, 101, 104, 113, 116; returns to Canada, 146; takes historic photographs on Málaga–Almería road, 76, 149; unified blood transfusion service, 58, 64, 92

Soccoro Rojo Internacional (SRI), 23, 28–9; backs Bethune's plan for mobile blood transfusion service, 24; Bethune proposes unified blood transfusion service to, 55; hospital in Almería, 72, 75, 83; supplies location and staff for Instituto, 26

socialized medicine, 10–11, 142

Sorensen, Henning, 21, 23, 38, 92, 122, 156; accompanies Bethune to battle of Guadalajara, 95; acts as Bethune's interpreter, 20, 56, 59, 99–100, 112, 113; critical of Kajsa Rothman, 112; given rank of captain in Sanidad Militar, 62, 63; goes with Bethune to Paris, London, and Barcelona, 24, 26, 27, 59, 153; goes with Bethune to Marseille, 57, 59, 116, 153; helps convince Bethune to return to Canada, 114; informs members of Instituto of reorganization of Sanidad Militar, 113–14; joins in writing complaint about Bethune to Communist Party of Canada, 112; leaves Instituto and joins Sanidad Militar, 112, 113–14; meets Bethune in Madrid, 18, 19, 20; photographs of, 19, 26, 38, 56, 121, 123, 143; returns to Canada, 146; serves as liaison officer for Instituto, 31, 63, 116; travels with Bethune to Guadarrama Mountains, 36

Spence, Benjamin, 27, 58, 114, 122, 131. *See also* Committee to Aid Spanish Democracy (CASD)

Spry, Graham, 13, 19